Secrets of
Creative
Visualization

Secrets of Creative Visualization

Phillip Cooper

SAMUEL WEISER, INC.

York Beach, Maine

First published in 1999 by
Samuel Weiser, Inc.
P.O. Box 612
York Beach, ME 03910-0612
www. weiserbooks.com

Library of Congress Cataloging-in-Publication Data

Cooper, Phillip.
   Secrets of creative visualization / Phillip Cooper.
     p. cm.
     Includes bibliographical references and index.
     ISBN 1-57863-102-5 (pbk. : alk. paper)
      1. Imagery (Psychology) 2. Visualization. 3. Creative ability.
   I. Title.
   BF367.C65 1999
   153.3′2—dc21   98–51029
                    CIP

EB

Cover photo by Paulo De Andrea
Cover design by Ed Stevens

Typeset in 11 Point Galliard

Printed in United States of America.

08 07 06 05 04 03 02 01 00 99
10 9 8 7 6 5 4 3 2 1

The paper used in this publication meets all the minimum require-
ments of the American National Standard for Permanence of Paper
for Printed Library Materials Z39.48-1984.

Inspiration

Somebody said that it couldn't be done
But he, with a chuckle, replied,
That maybe it couldn't but he would be one
Who wouldn't say so till he'd tried.

So he buckled right in, with a trace of a grin
On his face, if he worried he hid it,
And started to sing, as he tackled the thing
That "couldn't be done," and he did it!

Kenneth Horne[1]

---

[1] Kenneth Horne, *Somebody Said That It Couldn't Be Done* (Kings Langley, England: Paper Publications, 1995). Used by kind permission.

Table of Contents

Part Four: CREATIVE VISUALIZATIONS

List of Figures

Preface

I believe that everybody has power, or rather, access to power. There are no restrictions on how much power you use or how often you use it. In order to gain anything, you must exert some effort, you must try. So it is with power. If you want it, you must make the effort. If you want creative visualization to work, you must practice the art. If you want solid results, you have to do something to achieve them.

Life pours out energy, energy that can transform your life, bring success, happiness, and the fulfillment of your wildest dreams. Yet nothing will change unless you make some effort to accept and use this power.

You can have whatever you wish, but you must make the effort. Don't sit around accepting life's handouts and putting up with circumstances. Make the effort. Any effort (no matter how small) to contact power and any real desire backed up by action is bound to improve things. Don't sit down and do nothing; stand up. Assert yourself and realize that life is constantly offering you a chance to better yourself. Within every problem is a solution. That is how you identified the problem in the first place—by seeking the solution. You don't have to be an active practitioner of complex magical lore to make sweeping changes, but you do have to be active. This very special book of creative visualization is devoted to those who dare to act, and thereby claim the right to true living.

—P. Cooper, 1999

Introduction

Creative visualization is not difficult to learn and can give an alternative perspective on an otherwise predetermined future. It is possible to shape and control reality through the use of creative visualization and inner-mind power. This reshaped reality, in turn, interacts directly with the universe.

The path to success starts and ends with yourself. Your thoughts, needs, and desires have led you to the discovery of this book. Those same thoughts can bring you success in ways you never dreamed possible. Although this is a special book, it is not, in itself, magical. Nor do I pretend that the mere possession of it will alter your life. Its secret lies in your ability to grasp and apply the paradigms given herein. Once grasped and applied, they can begin to shape your future and hence your reality.

With this in mind, I have written this book to give you the very best in mind-power techniques that can be used successfully to shatter the illusion of matter and manifest your heart's fondest desires. To this end, your venture into magical lore will be highly focused, although, of necessity, we will look at certain esoteric facts so that you may have a complete picture of magical practice. Any "theoretical" work, however, is confined to that which is essential to the task at hand. It is, however, essential that you study and absorb this lore, as it is vital that you understand certain facts before your practical work can be fully effective. This lore, forming as it does an essential background to correct procedure, is often left out of self-help books. Here it is given in full. Study it carefully.

Part
One

The Cosmic Scheme

Chapter 1

In Search of Power

This is not a book about magic; it is a book that gives you magical paradigms and mind-power techniques to help you solve life's problems. I encourage you to put aside all preconceived ideas and forget what you may have been told or been led to believe. Read this chapter with an open mind and think about what you are reading. I do not insist that you accept these ideas without question; this would be silly and dogmatic. Instead, question these ideas, but do not reject them out of hand. Not only are they correct and based on truth, they will also work, given the chance.

Your Quest for Personal Power

The word "power" has become synonymous with brute force and oppression. And why not? For most of our history, those "at the top" have ruled, directed, and even abused those "at the bottom." Small wonder that people have given up believing that discretion is the better part of valor and accepted a reversal of the "fight-flight" paradigm that assumes that power is best left to those who know how to manage our lives.

Each day, we place ourselves in situations where the primitive, yet still-powerful, reactions of either "fight" or "flight" are repressed, to emerge only as a frustrated tapping of the fingers, a biting of the tongue, or erratic driving. If you are aware of your own emotional biases and wish to enhance either your self-assertion or self-restraint, then this book will help you achieve this. Moreover, it will demonstrate the massive extent to which conditioning is inflicted upon you by yourself and others.

While self-styled moguls struggle to hold the reins of power or jostle for social position, some individuals choose to tread an alternative path, going in search of a different kind of power—an alternative to oppression and a way to freedom. Who are these people and what motivates them to deviate, often at great personal risk, from the accepted norm? History gives but a scant account of such seekers, while many who discovered the truth, kept silent. Yet there are those who rose to prominence and, despite the risks, left a legacy of pointers and valuable clues as to where power may truly be sought. One such person was the Nazarine—Jesus.[1]

It is important to realize that, if there ever was such a man as Jesus, he taught only the truth concerning power and our inherent ability to use this to our advantage. Indeed there have been many such prophets, people of wisdom, and teachers. Each sought to *know*; each one discovered power; each one chose to teach the truth of our role in the universe. For a variety of reasons, some still valid today, they taught by parable, by allegory, or by riddles, rather than by stating things directly. This was not done to make people look foolish or to make them feel inferior, but to stimulate their minds in a rather special way and to conceal certain facts from those who would use these secrets to harm others. Remnants of this style are seen in the teachings of modern esoterics.

Central to all such teaching is the insistence that there is an overall intelligence or creative force known as "God" and that this force can be contacted by humans. The existing con-

[1]Jesus, or someone whom "Saint" Paul chose to call Jesus, set up a small charismatic cult and managed to get himself martyred. In fact, this was quite common at the time. The late Roman Empire suffered from a plethora of mystics, charismatics, prophets, and soothsayers. Jesus may have been one of many, or perhaps a composite character assembled from a number of stories. Paul never claimed to have met him, although he created a religion in his name. Even so, there are many grains of wisdom scattered throughout the New Testament.

cept of God, I assure you, is of no real value. It is inaccurate and misleading.

Everything in creation is alive, though you may not think it so. Even a supposedly dead stone has an active dimension. It is not solid, in the truest sense of the word. It moves constantly. Indeed, science has proven that so-called solid objects consist of tiny particles known as molecules. Moreover, in any one type of material, all molecules are the same. The only difference between, say, lead and gold, or water and wine, lies in the type of molecule of which each consists. Lead and gold have different molecules; therefore, they *are* different. However, what makes one type of molecule different from another? And why are they so different? The answer lies in the structure of the molecule.

Each molecule contains atoms which, in turn, consist of electrons revolving around a nucleus, rather like a miniature solar system. The number of electrons in each atom determines the essential nature, qualities, and characteristics of the atom. For instance, hydrogen has only one electron. It is highly flammable and can be explosive. If you add one more electron to the atom, making a total of two, you produce helium. This gas is not only heavier than hydrogen, it is also inert. A single electron has thus made a vast difference in the end product. With the addition of one electron, a hydrogen atom becomes helium. This may seem an oversimplification. Nevertheless, it happens to be true. Moreover, this observation raises some interesting questions about the possibility of "transmutation." Perhaps the attempts of alchemists to transmute lead into gold were not as silly as some would have us believe. What if Christ in fact changed water into wine by knowing about and applying an ability to change energy patterns, thereby effecting physical change?[2]

Every atom is held together by energy. Through this energy, often termed electricity or magnetism, the atom *lives*. You do not need to stretch your imagination very far to realize that, since all matter is composed of atoms, everything in creation is

---

[2]Gerald J. Schueler, *Enochian Physics: The Structure of the Magical Universe* (St. Paul, MN: Llewellyn, 1988), p. 141.

alive through its innate energy. The entire universe is nothing more or less than inert matter activated by power or life energy. The appearance, characteristics, and properties of a substance are therefore governed by the nature of its molecules, which, in turn, conform to the energy patterns within its atomic structure. From a scientific point of view, you could say that everything in existence is governed by energy patterns. Power (energy) therefore shapes and controls matter (molecules). Not only is the universe alive with power, it is governed by precise laws, even though it may appear to be quite chaotic.

Since the dawn of civilization, certain individuals have been instinctively aware of these laws, even though life appeared to be ruled by pure chance. If power exists, and if that power conforms to laws, then there must be "something" behind that order. What caused the order in the first place? Who or what created matter and then gave it form according to precise laws? Such thoughts have shaped the entire history of the human race, although not always for the best.

Certain individuals, through observation and contemplation, arrived at the idea that there must be something behind the order. Put yourself in the position of a man or woman living several thousand years ago. They knew nothing of the atomic theory, yet their instincts told them that there was power and order, and that there ought to be ways of contacting and utilizing them.

It is an integral part of human nature to personify intangibles, to prefer dealing with anthropomorphic images rather than abstractions. We see evidence of this, even today, in all sorts of phenomena, from beliefs in dwarfs, fairies, "little people," spirit guides, and Big Hairy Monsters (BHMs), to the Loch Ness monster, UFOs, and aliens, which may result from the pathology of a space-age psychosis or may be purely fictitious creations of the mind. Such things may simply be part of a complex two-way communication between the mind, which is, in itself, capable of being perceived by others, and some sort of alternate reality.

Humankind did, and still does, build mental images, although this tendency is often misunderstood and abused. Ancient men and women recognized power, knew that it was controlled by certain laws, and set out to contact that which had caused it. In their minds, primitive people reasoned that the source of this power must be a superbeing who lived "out there," beyond the stars or in some "other world" beyond the physical. This kind of thinking led them to conceive an image of this cause which, in keeping with the human need to personify concepts, became "God," or, to be more precise, the gods. Thus, the best place to begin our investigation of this power is with the alleged source of all power, God.

The Source of Power

In what kind of God do you believe? Do you believe in one God, or do you, as do many magic-minded people, believe in many gods? This is not a trick question. There are several possibilities:

- You may totally reject God or any such entity;
- You may not be really certain, but think that there is "something" responsible for life; or
- You may be convinced that there is a God or gods.

How many people have bothered to analyze the concept of God in an effort to discover what this entity is? Let me assure you, most people do not bother, although such questions are a vital part of personal understanding. By questioning, you often discover far more than the obvious. Make this a new rule in your quest for personal power. God is not beyond the question. How are you to understand the apparent source of power and your relationship with it if you do not question? If you really want to learn about something, you must ask questions, otherwise you will remain in the dark.

I should state at the outset, for those of you who are doubters, that I am not trying to convert you to Christianity, or any other ism or religion. This is the technique used in certain "mind power" books, and although there is some merit in it, I assure you that this is not my aim. That said, ask yourself why you doubt the existence of a God or gods. It may be for one of several reasons:

- You may be sick and tired of the indoctrination you received in early life and are reacting against it.

- You may secretly blame God for all the problems of the world, or for your own personal problems, and feel that God appears either too remote to be concerned or totally uninterested in whether you live or die.

- Deep down, you may believe, but fearing ridicule and in order not to be classified as a "jerk," you deny the possibility of a God.

- You may simply have rejected the thesis out of hand, without any serious thought.

- After serious consideration and a weighing of all available data, you may have arrived at the logical conclusion that God is simply an unsubstantiated myth. In short, you may have decided that God is unscientific, unprovable, and therefore nonexistent.

It is not important what your reasons are for rejecting the concept of God. It is only important that you know what they are. More important, you will be pleased to know that, no matter what your reasons, you are partially correct. In fact, I can state categorically that the presently accepted concepts of God are not only wrong, but show a marked lack of understanding of the true nature of power. In short, God, as commonly perceived, simply cannot exist. There is, however, another answer.

For those of you who believe in God, there are also some questions to be answered. You may believe in God for a number of reasons.

- You may never have really thought about it, but since most people believe in God, you go along in order not to be "different."

- You may have been taught not to question religious "truths," so you accepted God and the inevitability of "God's Will."

- You may simply have assumed that there must be *something* behind creation, therefore it must be God.

- You may be magic-minded or follow a pagan tradition that seeks to contact the gods.

- Having thought about it, you may be utterly convinced of the existence of God.

If you have thought about your belief in God or the gods, you will also be pleased to know that, whatever your reasons, you are also partially correct in your assumption that there is a God or gods. By now, I'm sure you are thinking to yourself: "Does he really know what he is talking about? First he tells us that there is no God or gods. Then he says that there is." Before you put this book down in confusion, let me explain: God (or gods) are whatever you think they are. Yes, that's right: *think*.

Since the beginning of our appearance on this planet, we have sought to better ourselves, either through sheer brute force and ignorance or by looking to the stars. Long ago, people realized that there was "something" behind life, something that could be contacted. That contact was first made in a personal sense. In other words, it was assumed that the power of creation was controlled by a "superbeing" beyond the comprehension of mere mortals. This primitive idea of the gods was later replaced by the concept of a single God. A human image of power was thus formed, or to be more correct, a superhuman image. Clearly, men and women invented the image of God. God did not invent men and women.

The reason there are so many gods, or so many different versions of God, is that each person has a different point of view and sees God in a different way. It should be remembered, however, that God is simply an image that exists only in our minds. Of what does this image consist? It consists of power in the form of life energy, power that conforms to precise laws and has intelligence, power that can be molded by thoughts—your thoughts. Ancient people conceived an image in their mind and then believed this to be true. This is still done today and, more importantly, these beliefs have physical effects, as you will see.

Both believers and nonbelievers should think carefully about the image of God they hold in their minds, or their image of any other "external" entity. Your beliefs color your life. You must be most careful, therefore, to have the right image— the right image for you, that is. The laws of the cosmos simply state that whatever you hold in your mind as true, is true. A realistic attitude toward God and God-power is thus an essential prerequisite for self-understanding.

An unquestioning belief in God and an absolute denial of God's existence are both simply a waste of time. A proper use of the image of God is, however, a powerful means to achieving results in a physical sense. First realize that there is power, energy, call it what you will and that this force pervades the entire universe. A good definition of this power is *life*. This life-energy is contained in all things, from a plain rock to a fully grown human being. In addition, this power conforms to precise laws. Many of these are far beyond our understanding; others are more obvious. It is almost as though Nature were controlled by a cosmic "clock" which, at precise times, turns energy on and off. You can see this in spring when, from apparently lifeless wood, new leaves start to appear. Unless the tree is really dead, this happens every year during spring—not summer or autumn, but spring, year after year. What causes this? Chemical reactions? If it is a chemical reaction, what causes the chemical reactions in the first place? The answer: the laws governing the cosmic tides of energy. It is, however, very easy to believe that there is some "being" behind this known as God or, if you are a pagan, "nature spirits." Ancient people had no conception of magical science or astrology (which is the science of charting cosmic-energy flow), so they assumed that the phenomenon was caused by "someone"—God.

It is so very easy to build mental images to explain the impossible or that which is not understood. It is even easier to build a personified image. Look at your own image of God. Either it is abstract (pure light, for instance), or it is more personal (a man in flowing robes up in heaven). In either case, you have an image and the more you think about it, the clearer it becomes. Try it for yourself. I will show you how in a moment.

Mental images have a profound effect on the mind, in particular the inner mind, of which I will say more later. Suffice it to say here that the type of mental image you hold is shaping your life, for better or for worse. Such is the power of images. This fact is well known to practitioners of magic, who make use of what are known as telesmatic images.[3] The art of constructing images could fill an entire book and is, in any case, beyond the scope of this work. It is enough for our purposes that there was an early realization of the use of power through images, a realization used by esoteric workers.

The most common mistake made when dealing with images is failing to recognize the image for what it is. When this happens it can cause unwanted effects and can give the image power in the wrong way. Any knowledgeable practitioner of magic knows that it would be stupid to give a telesmatic image the power to ruin your life. Yet we grant God this power through ignorance. The net result is that God is a confusing and contradictory concept. If you have ever read the Bible, you will know this.

On an individual level, your image of God (or lack of one) is extremely important. Whatever you conceive God to be will have a profound effect on your life, of this there can be no doubt. Remember that God is a special kind of image. Your image of God is your concept of what total power is. Moreover, whatever you believe the capability of total power is will have an effect on your life through the image you have adopted. The wrong image can produce the wrong result. Think carefully about your image or concept of what God is, or is not, to you. In this lies a major key to success in life. In

---

[3]Working with telesmatic images is fully discussed in *Inner Traditions of Magic* by William G. Gray (York Beach, ME: Samuel Weiser, 1978).

what kind of God do you believe? You will find that most of what is happening, or failing to happen, in your life is in keeping with this key belief. The lesson is therefore to think about this important image, realizing that your concept of God is whatever you wish it to be and that you can change the image to suit your needs. In short, *you can build a better relationship with power by altering its image.*

Establishing Contact with Power

A realistic way of establishing contact with power is to relax and then consider the natural cosmic scheme in order to attune your mind. Consider the fact that energy exists in everything, that it conforms to precise laws and thereby provides an intelligence behind life. Realize and accept that these laws are not restrictive, but creative. Moreover, whereas Nature simply creates, you have the free choice to create whatever you wish. The abundant flow of life-energy will always seek to assist you, whatever your motives. It is, therefore, totally beneficial, because it always supplies power that your inner mind can use according to your beliefs. Power is yours; it flows freely, without restriction and without end. To form a link with this power you must simply build a bridge between it and you. That bridge may be constructed in many ways. By far the best way however, is to construct a personified image and forge a relationship with it.

Think first about the sheer vastness of the universe and the enormous quantity of power that exists within it. Whatever created this power must itself be powerful beyond all conception. This power did not create itself, but was brought into being by universal intelligence—not a fixed and inflexible intelligence, but a self-generating intelligence, so that creation could continue freely within the laws of the cosmos. These laws allow maximum creativity, seeking not to control or restrict, but rather to provide channels along which power may flow freely into physical form. Universal intelligence therefore provides power, together with an incalculable number of paths along which power may flow. It would be wrong to assume, imply, or believe that this intelligence does not give—totally.

It is not difficult to approach this intelligence, nor does this require the intervention of a mediator. You are part of creation; you have the ability to create; you are in constant contact with this intelligence. Until now, your image of this contact has restricted your ability to enhance your life and to create whatever you need. In short, you have been led to believe that universal intelligence, or God, was far removed, and therefore unreachable. Or you have accepted the "traditional" images of God or the gods, which are, by their very nature, inadequate, inaccurate, and useless to you as an individual.

To think of God in human form, it is not necessary to conceive of him as a wise old man sitting in heaven, although, if it helps, you may use this approach, provided that you do not build negative human traits into the image. If your image of God takes a human form, treat this as a totally beneficent person who always assists in practical ways and who answers all questions truthfully. Be sure, however, to make the image completely positive and trustworthy. How? By believing it to be so. Alternatively, a nonhuman image may be used with equal success. Simply by accepting the truth that universal intelligence seeks only to create in perfect harmony and wants you to discover the truth and attain you heart's desires, you will build that all-important bridge.

Before performing creative visualization, or whenever you have free time, relax and think about *your* image of God along the lines suggested. If your image is of a person, converse with it. Ask questions and expect answers. Ask for assistance in overcoming problems and expect results. Trust this image, believe in it, and, with the passing of time, it will prove itself in many ways. The more you use this image and the more you become involved with it, the better the results will be. Exactly the same idea applies to the "nonhuman" method of contacting God. Although you may visualize God as simply intelligence without form, or simply a bright light, this does not preclude the fact that you must establish a personal contact with the image. It is *contact* that you are seeking, in the highest sense of the word. It is impossible for me to describe in any detail a precise way for you to build up contact, either through the use of personal images or through abstract connections. Each of you must do this in your own way. God, in the truest sense, is different for each individual. This is yet another reason why religious systems fail. They are too impersonal and extremely rigid. By thinking about God in a realistic light and by devoting some time to seeking contact with this powerful intelligence, you are bound to gain in the widest possible way.

Your image of God can make your life a misery if you believe in the wrong image. Conversely, your God can transform your life and give you real power. The sublime truth of the matter is that, by changing the image, you change your life. Science has been trying to understand life for centuries. You now have one of the great secrets! *Use* it!

Chapter 2

Beliefs Shape Reality

The cosmic scheme and its laws do not seek to punish you, make you pay for your "sins," or force you to comply with destiny. They seek only to impart perfection, and they never fail in this. Your beliefs are the key. Not only have they shaped your life so far, they will continue to do so. So what can you do to improve your life? The answer lies in two directions and neither is as difficult as you may think.

The first course of action is to realize that your existing beliefs do indeed have a powerful effect on your life. Think carefully about your beliefs. The more you think about them, the more you will be surprised by the negative ideas you hold within your mind. Some of you will recognize this immediately; for others it may take time. If you persist, however, you will discover the truth about your mental images and be able to rid yourself of those that are negative. How? Once the truth dawns, it is like a breath of fresh air. It fires you up and spurs you on to better things. As a result, old beliefs will give way to new and, of course, your inner mind will respond accordingly.

Your purpose in buying this book is, presumably, to seek and acquire power. The truth of the matter is that you already have power, although you are probably not aware of it. More important, this power is working for or against you, without your knowledge. In your search for this power, there are certain facts that you need to consider. We will look at these in detail.

As you have learned, it is important to forge a link with your own personal image of God. In other words, build a bridge between yourself and this creative source. Part of our conditioned thinking is a presumption that we must fight, sweat, and strain against impossible odds before we can be truly successful. Preconditioned thinking exists everywhere and dominates human life. It motivates men and women to act in the most absurd ways. It restricts their vision and, therefore, their potential.

Your deeper thoughts—for example, those that are dominant in your mind and that you believe to be true—are responsible for shaping your life and will go on shaping it until you change them. Put quite simply, whatever you believe to be true, is true. Your beliefs, therefore, control your future.

I said earlier that you already have power. Part of that power lies in your ability to believe. Do not dismiss this or accept my words without thought. Think about it. Consider also the words of a wise man named Christ. He gave us a great truth when he said, "If thou canst believe, all things are possible to him that believeth" (Mark 9:23).[1] You will notice that the statement is quite specific. It claims "all things" to be possible. There is no distinction made between good things and bad things nor are other limits defined. All things are implied, and all things meant.

Consider also the biblical statement, "Therefore I say unto you. What things soever ye desire, when ye pray, believe that ye receive them, and ye shall have them" (Mark 11:24). Yet another reference to the power of belief.

This has important implications and far-reaching consequences, for, if beliefs do indeed come true, there are two possibilities: Your inherent beliefs are working either for or against you, regardless of whether you are aware of this or not. It follows that you must question your own beliefs most carefully. If these are wrong and not in your best interests, you have a powerful force working against you. Now can you see why things do go wrong in life? No outside entity or force causes these things to happen. You do it yourself, through your own beliefs.

---

[1]This, and all following biblical quotes, are from the authorized King James Version of the Bible.

What *do* you believe in? Ask yourself this very important question, for it has a great bearing on your potential, and also on your future. Whatever has happened to you so far in your life is directly related to your own beliefs and you will continue to create your own future in accordance with these beliefs— that is, until you change them. If beliefs cause things to happen, it naturally follows that if you change these beliefs, you will change the future. Your entire future happiness is literally in your own hands.

It is so very easy to blame externalities. You have been conditioned to do so. From now on, however, you must not blame fate, luck, or even the gods. In fact, do not blame anything. Far better to look within, at your own thinking. The first rule of all meaningful philosophy is "man, know thyself." This "knowing" is a realization of what you really are, free from inherited beliefs and accepted concepts that have not been examined. In other words, you must move past artificially imposed barriers to your thinking and enter a new state of awareness. You must extend yourself into dimensions that have few purely human occupants. Think of it as a new birth. Indeed it has been likened to being "born again," to entering the "Kingdom of Heaven" or inner life. This latter point is also very relevant to your future. Since birth, you have been given values, standards, and ideals, together with a whole host of ideas that have been accepted— in other words, believed. These come from parents, teachers, priests, relatives, and friends, to name but a few. Is there any reason to suppose that the ideas and beliefs to which they subscribed were actually true? Even if some of them were, are they necessarily true for you? How many of the things you have been taught have now been proven wrong, even though they were held to be absolute? Not very long ago, we were led to believe that penicillin could cure all manner of afflictions. The result—we became immune to it.

Fear is one of the greatest problems in the world, yet the world is still ruled by it. This is the environment into which you were born and in which you were given the "rules." The net result is that each of you may have any number of "inner" problems. Deep down, you know what the truth is, and you desperately seek to express that truth. In direct opposition, you have a host of incorrect beliefs, together with all manner of other accepted values and standards that were given to you at birth. Not only do these cause actual problems, in a physical sense, they also cause inner strife. You, like most people, are being pulled simultaneously in two opposite directions. This leaves you with a choice. The real problem lies in the fact that you were not aware that this choice existed, due to the over-whelming number of negative belief patterns which, for you, make up the "obvious."

Consider the following paradigm of the difference be-tween supposed "good" and "evil," and consider how "tradi-tion" explains it. It describes a battle between God and the devil, representing the forces of light and darkness struggling for supremacy. Look at this logically. Does it seem likely, on the face of it, that the all-creative, all-knowing, all-seeing God would be stupid enough to create evil in the first place? Re-member, God, we are told, is perfect and cannot make mis-takes. Obviously, something is wrong with this concept. How did God ever miss seeing this, *before* the fact? Is God imper-fect? The answer, if there is to be such a thing as God, is no. What *is* imperfect is our image of God, as already explained. It should also be noted that the image of the devil was created to epitomize evil. The problem is that this image was given more power than was given by the paradigm to God. Think about this and look a little deeper at these things. The central para-digm is that God created *all things*. If he did, he must have cre-ated the devil as well.

The truth of the matter lies, once again, in the images constructed to represent the idea of good versus evil and the resultant belief in the image as an *actual* being. In truth, there is no such division between good or evil. It is all a question of choice and perspective. What is good for one person may well be bad for another. Think about this carefully. Who has the right to say that something is good or that it is bad? This is a presumption. Worse still, this distinction is an infringement on your right to think and decide for yourself. It impugns your vital obligation to look at life, and think for yourself, and set the standards by which you will live.

The original conceptions of good and evil are of tribal and religious origins and belong to a long-dead past. Time marches on, yet the same standards prevail here in the 20th century. They are still believed to be true and are accepted without question. The result is that men and women seek to destroy all those things defined as "evil" while, at the same time, limiting themselves to those things defined as "good." An example of this sort of stunted thinking can be seen in the "holy" wars, in which perfectly innocent people were slaughtered so that "good" could triumph. Here is a classic case of the powers of good doing something evil. If you were to choose a path different from that of Christianity, would you consider a war waged against you justified? No, of course you would not. So who is right—the church or the infidel?

It all comes down to a question of different points of view—or at least it should. Because of the limited thinking of those who, long ago, defined good and evil, one faction, considering itself to be in the right, felt justified in wiping out those unfortunates who thought differently. The same thing happens even today. Acknowledging those different points of view is important because it is our right and our obligation to choose for ourselves what we believe to be right. Yet, all too often, we do not exercise this right because "right" and "wrong" have already been defined for us. The ultimate stupidity occurs when we carry this misguided concept over into our creative work.

It is one thing to advise people in a general sense as to what *may* be good or evil, and to offer alternatives. It is another to define rigid laws and then impose them on others. It is worse still to invent images to convey our own personal concepts (images such as that of the devil) and insist that others act upon them. Those familiar with the Bible will remember the story of Christ saying, "Get thee behind me, Satan" (Matthew 17:23). This implies that there is some sort of creature—Satan or the Devil—who has nothing better to do other than to tempt people away from the supposed straight and narrow. This is grossly incorrect on two counts. In the search for the higher self, which requires maximum contact with the power of the inner mind, concentration is vital, hence the need to be shut off from the world. But remember that the material world reacts to you in accordance with your beliefs. If those beliefs are wrong, their effects will also be wrong. It is, therefore, vital to shut incorrect beliefs out of your mind for periods of time. The time required for this retreat will depend very much on your own individual needs. Not everyone can or should retreat completely from the world. For some it is right; for others it could be a mistake. Personal choice is always the governing factor in these matters.

The idea of Satan or the Devil may, indeed, be a valid one. It is not correct, however, in the way that religion would have you believe. Christ was not dealing with an entity known as Satan. He was merely using a little-known technique for dealing with the inner mind. This technique is known as the art of telesmatic images. A deliberately manufactured humanoid symbol such as that of Satan, which has grown through ignorance into a force that represents the undesirable effects of the now-outmoded belief/material/reaction relationship, is, in fact, of little use. You can still use this personified image, if you so desire, but only with certain reservations.

Notice, on the other hand, how useful this can be. In your imagination, you can command this symbol to do certain things, such as "get thee behind me." In other words: "I banish you from my mind, thereby removing from my reality all that you represent."

If you study this technique carefully you will begin to see its obvious advantages over other methods. Speedy communication with parts of your inner mind are possible; the results, therefore, are likely to be just as quick. From the opposite point of view, if you wish to use beneficial energies to realize some particular desire, build a mental image of the sort of "being" capable of accomplishing this on your behalf. It is a perfectly valid inner technique.

People believe in these images. Every Christian believes in some sort of devil paradigm. In magick, exactly the same problem exists. In fact, the same distinctions are applied and believed. We hear of "black" magic and "white" magic, or of angels and demons. It seems that the forces of "light" are in constant battle with the hordes of "darkness." Moreover, all this takes place in the vast arena of the universe with you as the prize. It is, in fact, a classic example of the good guys versus the bad guys so beloved of Hollywood film producers. But who will win?

The answer is that those who believe they will win, will win. Belief is probably the most powerful force in the universe. When you believe in helpful gods, the results are beneficial. When you change those beliefs, they change your circumstances so that they become detrimental. The gods did not change, nor did they seek to punish you. They were only images in your mind. Your beliefs changed and so did the images. But the beliefs came first. They gave rise to the gods who, in turn, were allowed to control your future. The gods may well shape your life, but since your beliefs shape the gods, we must conclude that they, in turn, shape your life. This is an absolute truth:

If thou canst believe — all things are possible.
—Mark 9:23

The rift between the material and the spiritual sides of life is akin to the distinction made in the good versus evil syndrome. And it is just as unreal. Your greatest problem is, and always has been, your misguided relationship with the material side of life. This is largely self-induced through lack of understanding and acceptance of the wrong ideals. It is my hope that this book will help set you straight and reveal the spiritual/material conflict for what it is — nonsense!

It is the height of folly to reject the material side of life for the spiritual. This is not the way to truth. You cannot reject the material, because you live in it and are of it. You must, therefore, learn to control your material reality by using natural laws. If you do not learn this control, chaos will ensue. Control is achieved by using the mind in ways that can be described as magical.

The part that belief plays in this cannot be overstressed. "Whatever you believe in your heart—so shall you be." This is a cosmic absolute—it cannot be altered. It must therefore be used or it will continue to function in the wrong way. Consider carefully the enormous impact that this law can, and does, have on your life. If you believe you are imprisoned in the "flesh" and must therefore "evolve" beyond it, what, in effect, are you doing? By believing that your body is a prison, you are setting up a chain of images that lead to events that will ensure that you in fact become a prisoner. Whatever you may believe, so shall you become. If you choose to believe that the "material" side of life should be rejected, by virtue of that belief you will accomplish just that—and you will be the poorer for it. This is made even more sad by the fact that this belief may not even be your own. It may belong to someone else. More to the point, it is simply *wrong*. Little wonder that such people are confused by life's problems. They seek an enigmatic path to a nonexistent spiritual state in a physical world. At the same time, they cause themselves and others much suffering and hardship.

The ordinary non-seeking individual has a similar problem, because the law of belief applies to everyone, regardless of who they are or what they consider themselves to be. More often than not, people are completely unaware of their inner beliefs. They have simply accepted them and are therefore plagued by problems to which there seem to be no solutions. They either resign themselves to fate, thinking, "That's life," or they blame other intangibles, such as God's will. Naturally, the problems persist. In fact, ideas like this only add fuel to the fire, because they prevent an understanding of the truth and preclude any questioning of beliefs. When you consider that beliefs make things happen, and that these beliefs and their effects are being projected into the future, is it any wonder that fate, karma, or divine punishment seem to be valid concepts? The truth, however, is that each individual is actually creating their own future, in accordance with their innermost beliefs.

From a magical point of view, those who choose to deny the material, even if they consider themselves to be enlightened or "initiated" adepts, are subject to the same law. They search for the unobtainable, when even their own symbol, the Tree of Life, tells them that reality must first be sought in the physical. They try to reject the material, not realizing that the first true initiation is one of learning to control their physical environment. The Tree of Life is rooted in solid earth. The law states that, unless you understand and learn to control the physical side of life, you are not going to gain much from your so-called spiritual searching.

Magick and creative visualization start by looking at the self, by learning the truth about life on Earth, and by first being practical. In other words, learn how to control the physical side of life.

Chapter 3

Discovering the Real You

For centuries, humankind has sought power. Few ever found its secret, because they have looked in the wrong places. Obsessed by this search, they failed to look in the most obvious place—within themselves. Christ tried to tell them, as did others, but they paid no heed. They were told to seek the Kingdom of God first: "But rather seek ye the kingdom of God, and all these things shall be added unto you" (Luke 12:31). Yet they sought in the physical domain and presumed to impose a worldly kingdom on others: "Neither shall they say, Lo here! or, lo there! for, behold, the kingdom of God is within you" (Luke 17:21). They were told that the kingdom lay within themselves, yet they looked outside. Such is the fate of the foolishly "wise." Mystery was heaped upon mystery and error piled upon error in the search for power. Yet power still seems to elude the searcher.

If no other good comes out of this book, you will have learned one of the greatest secrets of all time—that you have the ability to question and ask why. By asking this question, and by refusing to accept anything less than the truth, you will discover secrets that baffle the greatest minds. Question everything, especially that which is accepted as normal or presented as "fact."

In the search for power, we must follow the advice of wise people and look within ourselves rather than at the obvious. So what is it, within ourselves, that causes power to flow in accordance with our beliefs?

Have you ever thought about the *real* you? There are as many misconceptions about this as there are stars in the heavens. Yet, before you can claim and use power, you must discover the truth of yourself. It is, after all, this truth that can set you free, for knowing this truth means that wrong, self-limiting beliefs will no longer stand in the way of your ability to claim power.

Who or what are you? Throughout the ages, certain prophets, sages, and philosophers have tried to answer this. Unfortunately, communications in those bygone days were not particularly efficient, and the answers have come to us shrouded in mystery. Who or what are you? If you are perfectly honest with yourself in answering, your image of yourself will either agree with an established norm, whatever that may be for you, or it will be vague and unsatisfying. Perhaps we ought now to look more closely at you and your role in this cosmic scheme.

You are an eternal being who, in this life, has chosen to live on a physical planet, in a physical body. You are *not* your body. This is simply a vehicle that you leave behind after death—you continue forever. It's strange how many people actually fear death—or see it as an absolute end. Yet there is nothing to fear, for death is simply a transition to another state of existence. Life goes on, regardless of the death of your physical body. Death phobias are now quite common, however, and so deeply rooted in the minds of men and women that they result in an attitude of "doom." Why bother to live or try to achieve something better if you are already condemned? What is the point of trying when, apparently, there is nothing beyond death? These ideas are inaccurate concepts of what divinity is and how it functions.

Christ taught that we are eternal, and others have also testified to this. It is the only logical answer, for what is the point in living here on Earth, simply to perish and then cease to exist? Creation simply does not work like this, for creation seeks only to continue life, not exterminate it! In any case, no god would be sadistic enough to give life, then take it away. It simply does not make sense to presume that physical death is the absolute end. By the same token, to presume that you are forced to live here as a form of penance is also absurd. In fact, I defy anybody to prove that this is so. To subscribe to any doctrine that compels obedience is to limit yourself and restrict your potential. Although this has been an accepted pattern of thought since time immemorial, it is, nonetheless, untrue. You are eternal and you are also free to choose how and where to live—unless, that is, you believe otherwise.

Belief is the key to all things. It can make life easy or very difficult: "Whatsoever a person believeth in their heart—so shall they be." The word "be" is very important to the meaning of this verse. For, according to this true statement, we can "be" anything. Moreover, does it not make profound sense to "be" that which you really are and that which you really wish to be? Ask yourself, what do *you* wish to be? Do you wish to be a pathetic creature condemned to a life of misery and pain, ending in extinction or eternal torment? Or do you aspire to be powerful, creative, in control, and abundantly happy? There is really only one choice. And you have the right and obligation to choose, as you will see.

You are not your body. You simply use your body during your Earth-life. It is the most suitable vehicle for the environment in which you live. You also have a mind that can be used to think, to feel, and to evaluate impressions received from sight, touch, and taste. It is a marvelous mechanism—but it is not *you*. Think about something, then tell me who is doing the thinking. The answer is that you are—the real you. Never forget that the real you is not some shining, remote, angelic figure to be approached with awe and reverence. I know that this is the impression created by certain "adepts," but I tell you that this is wrong. The real you is simply *you*—the one who thinks. You can choose to think whatever you like. In fact, you can *do* anything you like. The only thing that prevents you from doing something successfully is your beliefs. Do you believe that you can walk on fire? Of course not. Yet, under hypnosis, you could.

You can think and, with these thoughts, you can create. How? Through the vast power and potential inherent in your own inner mind. Through this incredible part of your inner being, you have access to the vast resources of the universe, if you but knew it. This is the major problem of the human race. They have forgotten who they really are and of what they are truly capable. "Ye are Gods" (John 10:34). Christ knew this and so did others. Yet they were ignored. If you have accepted my reasoning so far, you will have reached a crossroads in your life. You can choose to go on listening to and accepting dogma, incorrect postulations, and unreal thinking, or you can start to think for yourself. If you do, there will be no turning back. You will learn the meaning of the word "freedom" and, more important, you will learn the beginnings of real creative living.

The truth of the matter is that you, exercising your free choice, can think creatively. In other words, you can think things into existence by using the power of your inner mind. There is nothing new in this. In fact, you are already doing it, and have been doing it throughout your life. The problem has been that you were not aware of doing it. You presumed, like everyone else, that life was predestined, or at least beyond your ability to control. How wrong you were.

Throughout your life, your beliefs have been active, made to work by this hidden ingredient, your inner mind. In short, everything you are today, everything that you experience, and everything that happens (for good or evil) is a direct result of your beliefs—beliefs that have been given life by your inner mind.

Look at the things in which you really believe. Have they come true? By this, I do not mean those things that you hoped might come true. I mean your deepest beliefs. Be honest. What do you expect from life? What do you anticipate is likely to happen over the next few weeks, months, or years? You already know what is likely to happen, based on what you believe to be true for you. This knowing is shaping your future as precisely as a computer works out a calculation. You, and no one else, are responsible for what happens next, because your innermost thoughts are shaping your future, using the vast potential of your inner mind.

Think about this. For, if your beliefs do indeed shape your future, there are two possibilities. Your beliefs may have been inherited from others and molded by parents, teachers, or society. Or they may be religious or devotional, in which case they have probably not been thought about. Yet these beliefs are molding your future, for all beliefs cause things to happen. Is it any wonder that you are not content with your life? On the one hand, you hope and wish for better things, yet these seem to elude you. You know what you wish to have, yet these objectives appear to be beyond your reach. Not knowing the truth, you may have presumed that these were "not for you" or that "fate" was against you. You may even have accepted the "fact" that you were "unlucky," blamed intangibles such as God, or accepted that the material side of life was to be rejected in favor of the so-called spiritual. You have, in fact, added to your original misconceptions and actually strengthened them. Little wonder that they continue to influence your life and so cause a rift within yourself. Part of you truly wishes to be abundantly happy and seeks to express itself fully. Part of you may know, deep down, that this is possible, while the other side of you inadvertently creates all manner of problems. The result is chaos, stress, uncertainty, hopelessness, and depression. Deep down, you wish only to be yourself and have those things that are truly yours, yet, on the outside, you appear to be at the whim of external forces that deny these things. These "external" forces do not exist. The real problem lies within yourself and those problems will, in fact, continue until you change your inner reality.

If beliefs have such power (and there can be no doubt that this is true), the answer to the problem must lie within the problem itself. All that you have to do is *think*. By "think," I mean "look at your beliefs," be rational about them, then change them for better ones. You are perfectly entitled to do so. The result is bound to be a change in circumstances, for it is a scientific fact that "As you believe—so you are."

Changing these old, outmoded beliefs is not difficult. It can be made considerably easier by adopting a more realistic outlook based on the truth rather than what only appears to be the truth. Learn to recognize who and what you really are, instead of what you think you are or merely consider yourself to be. Accept more realistic concepts of your role in life and of what can be achieved. Know that you are indeed "god-like" and that, therefore, you have "god-power," for this is literally true. Think like this and you will replace old and damaging beliefs with far better ones. Moreover, in view of the fact that beliefs always get results, you cannot fail to enhance your life in many ways.

Christ spoke of a "Kingdom of God" within ourselves. What sort of kingdom would you expect this to be? If it truly is a God-kingdom, then surely, in keeping with the real idea of God, anything is possible. In fact, we are informed that this is true. "But rather seek ye the kingdom of God, and all these things shall be added unto you" (Luke 12:31). All these things, not some of these things. All things is stated, all things meant. The message is quite obvious. This inner "kingdom" grants all wishes and all requests, without exception. Little wonder that Christ said: "Is it not written in your law, I said, Ye are Gods?" (John 10:34). Within every individual, there is a kingdom of God-power that can be used. That power lies in the vast potential of the inner mind.

You are, in reality, an indestructible entity who will live forever. You "live," at this point in time, on the planet Earth. You decided to live here in order to experience physical existence. You were not forced to come here by "sin" or through the workings of "karma." You chose this life. As an eternal being, you are creative. In other words, you can alter life to suit yourself by creating around yourself all that you wish to have. This creative process is activated by beliefs that, in turn, cause your inner mind to alter circumstances according to your needs. The more positive your beliefs, the more positive the results, for life seeks only to comply with your wishes— those wishes, that is, that are believed to be possible or true. This is the truth about life and, if you will begin to consider this instead of simply accepting dogmas and half-truths, I promise that you will know power in a way you never considered possible.

Chapter 4

The Incredible
Power of the Inner Mind

Having spent some time sweeping away superstitions and misconceptions, let's look at creative visualization in a realistic light. Creative visualization is a science—the science of understanding and using the vast potential of the inner mind. Certain prophets and sages have given us valuable clues to the vast potential of the inner mind. One such person was Christ. Christ is purported to have said, "But rather seek ye the kingdom of God, and all these things shall be added unto you" (Luke 12:31). He claimed that the kingdom of God lay within. "Neither shall they say, Lo here! or, lo there! for, behold, the kingdom of God is within you" (Luke 17:21). This is often interpreted to mean some far-distant part of the galaxy or some idealistic "Heaven" that we must seek by ridding ourselves of the supposed "evils" and "temptations" of the flesh. Nothing could be further from the truth. The truth is that we must first seek the kingdom that lies within. What kingdom and within what? The kingdom of God (power) lies within your inner mind. In other words, in your subconscious or preconscious mind. That is all that Christ was trying to communicate. He tried to communicate it in a way that could be understood by ordinary people (bear in mind that the idea of the subconscious was unknown in Christ's time). The word "within" may perhaps have meant more to Easterners, with their natural bent toward the mystical, but in fact it was simply another way of saying "inside the mind."

I will not go into Christ's statements in any depth, other than to point out that he must have known about inner-mind power, since he tried to teach this knowledge and, more to the point, to apply it. Christ was, if nothing else, a highly pragmatic man. Once you discovered the kingdom, he promised, "All things will be added unto you." All things. This is important, for there are no restrictions given or implied. Once you have discovered the kingdom, how do you go about using this power?

Again Christ had the answer. First, he taught in parables. Parables are simply short stories that conjure up pictures in the mind. Mental pictures have a profound effect on the inner mind! Second, he gave precise instructions in an easily understandable way, instructions like, "If thou canst believe, all things are possible to him that believeth" (Mark 9:23). Again, notice the word "all." The key to understanding inner power is, therefore, to be found in two ways: through imaginary pictures or symbols (visualization), and through belief. These are the two important paths to inner power that we will now examine and then apply.

Little is known of the inner mind, other than it does exist and that it exhibits some remarkable characteristics. Because our knowledge of it is somewhat limited, we tend to underestimate its potential, especially in pragmatic terms. Although "mind-power" books have gone a long way toward demonstrating this potential, modern practitioners of magick have largely ignored it, while religion has attempted to stamp out anything remotely related to the "world of the strange." Now is the time for people to realize that the inner mind does exist, that its potential is far beyond anything previously suspected, and, more importantly, that its potential can be proven and applied. Science has verified that will and mind power can interact directly with the universe. Furthermore, the use of these forces does not contravene the laws that govern life. This potential is available to anyone who is willing to look a little deeper at life, to move beyond the obvious. It is not necessary for you to have a degree in science or psychology in order to use this potential. The keyword to the inner mind is "simplicity." Those who wish to study it will find much that is complex, yet there is a fundamental thread of simplicity throughout. Life is, in reality, a simple affair. So too is the inner mind.

What do you think keeps your heart beating at precisely the proper rate, regardless of what you may be doing? What is it that makes your eyes blink automatically, digests your food, governs how much breath you take in, or makes you shiver when you are cold? What is it that controls tens of thousands of body cells, miles of nerves, and an incalculable number of bodily functions, without you having to think about these things? The answer is your inner mind. Think of the impossible task of having to control a minute fraction of these all by yourself. You could not and, even if you did achieve some success, there would not be enough time left to think or to do anything else. If you cut yourself, your inner mind immediately swings into action to stop the bleeding. This in itself is a major operation, involving many different bodily functions. But look what else happens. Having arrested the flow of blood, your inner mind sets about repairing the damage by healing the wound.

The point to remember is the sheer versatility of the inner mind, together with its ability to perform tasks that, if you think seriously about them, are nothing less than miraculous— even if they are ordinarily taken for granted. Controlling bodily functions is, however, only one aspect of this part of your mind. It has many other secrets and it is to these that we must now turn in our search for "unlimited" power.

By observation, it is possible to assume that something is responsible for healing, for automatic reflexes, and, of course, for stranger phenomena, such as "inspiration," telepathy, clairvoyance, or astral projection. That "something" is the inner mind, whose potential is far greater than you might suspect. A fair analogy might compare the inner mind to a vast computer. It controls thousands, if not millions, of different bodily functions, in the same way that any reasonable-sized computer would, say, in a factory or in a spacecraft. Like a computer, it is programmed to carry out certain tasks. In our case, it is programmed to look after your well-being and to protect you from harm. We all have "instincts" that warn us of danger or "feelings" that something is wrong. This is the inner mind acting in its protective capacity. But the inner mind executes two other types of "programming" as well. One deals with creative potential, the other with insight. It is to the former that we must turn if we are to master life's problems.

A computer can be programmed to do virtually anything, from running a line of complex machines to working out the most complex mathematical problems. The same computer can just as easily be programmed to detonate a hydrogen bomb. There are two points to bear in mind: it is the program that dictates what the computer will do or will not do, and the computer makes no distinction between beneficial and destructive programs. It simply acts on the instructions it is given. The computer could never be considered "evil," but a program can make it perform functions that fall under the heading of "evil." It is, therefore, what you put into the computer that really matters.

So, where is all this leading? Your inner mind is, in reality, nothing more or less than a "spiritual" computer. It is already programmed to look after your welfare, but it can be given additional instructions at any time. This is the real secret of creative visualization, because creative visualization is nothing more or less than the science of using the vast potential offered by your own inner mind to "reprogram" your life.

Regardless of what religion, education, science, or any "ism" or "ology" may present as fact or truth, the real truth is that we have a built-in computer with vast creative potential and unlimited power. At this point, you may have been prompted to ask, "If this is the case, why do we suffer so much misery and lack if we do indeed have this power?" In order to answer this, we must look a little more deeply into the inner mind and its workings.

Keep in mind the analogy of the computer. It too is very complex in its construction, yet its operation is really quite simple. Even young children can operate a computer quite easily, despite the fact that it took a genius to design it. Like a computer, the inner mind accepts and acts on instructions. It does not make moral judgments (such as what is right or wrong), nor does it accept instructions it cannot understand. So, in order to get the computer to react, you have to work within specific guidelines, in a specific "programming language." Some of these guidelines have already been mentioned.

With computers, you communicate by using a keyboard on which you type out instructions. Unless the computer can understand what you are trying to say, nothing will happen. The same problem exists with the inner mind, and for a very good reason. Your inner mind responds to thoughts, hence the idea given in mind-power books that thoughts are powerful things. This is not strictly true, however. Thoughts are merely a means of communicating with the inner mind. It is the inner mind that has the power and produces results. You think and the inner mind responds. This, in a nutshell, is what basic Magick is all about. Moreover, not every thought will get through to the inner mind, for the simple reason that, if they did, life would be just about impossible. Think about this carefully. Imagine the potential problems if every fleeting thought actually materialized? Unless you were a very positive-minded individual, you would not dare lose concentration. Life would be madness for most people, and most certainly a trial for the rest.

For this reason, the inner mind has a safety mechanism which allows only a specific kind of thinking to pass through. Ordinary thoughts are ignored completely, but this "special" thinking gets through. What is this special type of thought? Christ, and others, left us with valuable clues as to how we may use special thoughts in order to utilize the power of the inner mind. The teachings of these prophets are just as valuable today as they were in ancient times. Truth is truth. It is unalterable. It can be, and has been, buried by dogmatists and missed completely by those whose function it was to teach. This truth will now be given in 20th century terms.

Christ spoke of faith and belief. Faith and belief are special types of thought. They are focused, unwavering, and take no heed of the "obvious." They are like a beam of light that travels in a straight line, refusing to bend or to be blown off course. Many people say they believe that matters will get better, but do they really believe it? In most cases, the answer is no. Those same people may believe in all manner of self-restrictive ideas, yet they deny this basic truth. Our ideas about belief, therefore, are in need of further examination.

The absolute truth is that, whatever you believe to be true, is true. The more you learn of the powers of the mind, the more you will be convinced of this essential truth. The key to the riddle of life's problems, to the attainment of joy, fulfillment, and happiness, lies in your existing beliefs and in your ability to believe in better things. Remember, your inner mind knows no limits, no barriers, no restrictions. It is your "kingdom of God," to which you must turn for real power. When you do, power is always given, because it is the duty of your inner mind to serve you and to supply your every need. So why do things go wrong? Why is there so much misery? Why does luck, wealth, love, and happiness seem to elude people? The answer is quite simple—so simple that most people miss it or refuse to accept it. You must now think about this carefully. You will then be faced with a choice: either to go on accepting things as they are, while dismissing these ideas as nonsense, or to accept the challenge and start to change matters.

Belief influences the inner mind, which, in turn, seeks to make this belief factual. If your beliefs are negative, negative results occur, simply because your inner mind does not make moral judgments. In other words, if you really wish to believe in poverty, lack, pain, self-restriction, or crippling illnesses, your inner mind will seek to supply them.

Why? Because the law of free choice overrides everything. Your choice determines what happens—there is no other answer. Ignore the supposed "obvious" for a while—forever if possible! The simple truth, if you will but accept it, is that you have free choice to believe in whatever you wish. As a result of your belief, you will receive the consequence of your belief "pressed down and flowing over," for better or for worse, because your inner mind does not distinguish between what is right or what is wrong. It simply acts on the instructions given to it.

The one fact that emerges from all of this is that, if anything can be believed to be true, anything can become true. Why is this? Simply because your inner mind does not judge, evaluate, or take a moral point of view. It simply seeks to make true all that is believed to be so. If you believe in a Christian God and all that this implies, your inner mind will simply seek to bring this into your life. You have accepted a belief; your inner mind will seek to actuate this belief in physical terms. There are two main ways in which beliefs are formed. You may believe in the physical "facts" that you can see, touch, feel, or taste. Or you may believe in intangible things such as luck, fate, or the "way of things." Both types of things, if believed to be true, are true. However, by changing your beliefs, you are able to change the supposed facts. The two are linked together.

What happens when a person with an "incurable" illness suddenly gets better? That person refuses to accept the supposed "facts" of the matter—in other words, adopts a line of nonbelief. This refusal to accept the "inevitable" is, of course, a new pattern of belief. As a result, a new belief is accepted by the inner mind and a "cure" results. The important fact to emerge from this is that, if a thought is sustained, it becomes true. This is belief. It works because the inner mind does not know the difference between "fact" and "adopted fact." This is the key to success. From a physical point of view, you can look at life and believe what you see; it will therefore be "true." But because of the power of the inner mind, you can also choose not to believe in the "obvious" and adopt a different pattern of belief. This will also become true, because nonbelief in one set of facts implies belief in another. There is no such thing as pure nonbelief, if you think about it. To say, "I do not believe that" means that you believe that something is not true. Take the case of atheists. They will say that they do not believe in God, but what they really mean is that they believe that no

God exists—there is an important difference. We all believe in something, even if that belief is merely that something is not possible.

In order to change your life, therefore, you have to change your beliefs. There are two ways of doing this. You can simply accept a better belief, or you can practice believing in what you want. The former approach is never easy at first, but it can become so with practice. The latter approach is the one we will work with. There is no need to drive out old beliefs or to do battle with your soul. All you need to do is to adopt the scientific way of doing things.

How can you do this? How can your life be filled with abundance, happiness, love, and wealth? Read on.

Part
Two

Shaping Reality

Chapter 5

Relaxation and Affirmations

Creative visualization is the science of using the vast potential of the inner mind. This science rests on two assumptions: that the inner mind responds to beliefs, and that we can modify our beliefs. Have you ever tried to believe that something will happen, when the facts indicate that this is not possible? As an example, try believing that you will get a better job when there is really none available. Or try believing that you can acquire a very expensive car you cannot afford. First you will meet a barrier of objections based on "facts." These facts are being presented to you by your mind—your conscious mind. Your reason tells you that certain things are not possible. Where does it get this information? It gets it from your own memory which, in turn, resides in your inner mind. These memories, which prompt your conscious mind, are based on "facts" that you have accepted—in other words, believed.

Immediately, you can see a problem. If you want to change some aspect of your life—say, to have more money—you have to believe that this can happen. However, if deep within your inner mind there is an existing belief that this is not possible, the result is a stalemate that, but for the science of creative visualization, together with the flexibility of the inner mind, could well continue. For most people, this stalemate will continue until they realize that fate, destiny, luck, the "will of God or the gods" are nothing more than patterns of belief of the worst sort. Those who choose to look a little further than the supposed "obvious" will, sooner or later, start to question those beliefs and, given time, may eventually realize the truth.

The problem with the "facts" and the "obvious" is that these may or may not be true for the individual. The latter is usually the case. To be effective in creative visualization, you must learn to ignore the supposed facts in favor of a new line of thinking based on absolute truth that the facts can always be changed. This is quite simply due to the ability of the inner mind to produce these facts in the first place. It has the ability to alter the energy patterns within matter, so that they conform to your beliefs. It is therefore true that, if facts can be created, they can be changed. The "obvious" is therefore transient. It is a mistake to believe that it is unalterable. You may wish to change something; you may even hope with all your heart that this can be so. Yet you look at the obvious and believe that it cannot be changed, rather than listening to the facts with which your own mind presents you and believing these instead. Little wonder that nothing changes, for the obvious facts simply substantiate what you already believe to be true. However, as with all problems, the solution here lies within the problem itself. By changing your original beliefs for the better, you are bound to change the facts. More importantly, your conscious thinking will then substantiate this new belief. There is obviously a lot to be gained by this. But how do you change these beliefs in the face of so much opposition from your own mind?

At the beginning of this chapter, I stated that creative visualization rested on two assumptions. The first is your ability to change your beliefs. The second is the mechanism by which beliefs are accepted by your mind. Consider hypnotism. Hypnotism works by implanting a suggestion into the inner mind. When this is accepted—in other words, believed—everything changes in accordance with this new instruction. For instance, suppose that, during a hypnotic session, it is suggested that the subject is at the North Pole. Providing that the subject is willing to accept this suggestion, he or she will experience this as though it were true. In fact, the subject will be convinced to such a degree that he or she will actually see these new surroundings and experience the bitter cold. The hypnotist will notice no change in the surroundings, but the subject will behave as though he or she had actually been transported to the Arctic. It will be very real. For some reason, the conscious mind has been fooled. It has been bypassed, and it is this fact that gives the clue as to how you may change your beliefs and therefore your life.

Hypnotism works because the conscious mind is bypassed, leaving the hypnotist free to deal directly with the inner mind. During hypnosis, the subject is put into a deep trance in which he or she becomes still and calm. Creative visualization uses the same principle, but without using a hypnotic trance. Instead, access to the inner mind is achieved by using relaxation to calm and control the conscious mind, thereby avoiding the barriers that it would normally present. By relaxation, I do not mean watching the television or reading a book. I mean a deliberate relaxation of the body and mind. This is not difficult to do, but it does require practice until the technique becomes second nature.

It is vital that you learn how to do this. One of the biggest problems facing you is that you cannot control your conscious mind. By learning to do this, you will acquire power. An inability to do it can cause doubts, anxieties, worries, and uncertainties, all of which are guaranteed to make your creative work fail. The first rule of creative visualization is therefore:

$$Peace = Power$$

The more tranquil you are, the more you can control your conscious mind, the easier it will be for you to gain access to your inner mind. This formula gets results.

Preparation

The first step in creative visualization is to learn the art of relaxation. Before you can do this, you must find a quiet place where you will not be disturbed. If you have a spare room that can be used as a workroom, well and good. If not, use a bedroom. The main consideration is that you must be able to practice without being disturbed, for the simple reason that you cannot relax fully, or apply your mind completely to creative visualization, in a state of chaos or with part of your mind alert to the possibility of someone disturbing you. The whole of your mind must be on the work at hand. In order to do this effectively, the risk of interruption or distraction must be minimized. This may take a little ingenuity and some planning. It is, however, essential.

Relaxation

Learning to relax is easy. It requires no effort. Far from striving to control your body and mind, you have to learn to do the opposite. The technique of relaxation is one of letting go rather than of forcing something to happen. Find a chair and sit upright, arms resting on your lap. Close your eyes and direct your attention to your breathing. Breathe slowly in and out, without strain. Continue to do this for a few minutes, keeping your attention on your breathing. As you do this, you will find that thoughts enter your mind. Do not let these disturb you. Bring your attention back to your breathing. You will find that you are becoming calm and restful.

Now adopt this idea. When breathing out, imagine that you are letting go of tension and that problems are flowing away from you. Do not concern yourself with what these problems are. Just imagine that they are going away. You are letting them go. Conversely, while breathing in, imagine that power is flowing toward you and that you are becoming stronger and more able to control your life. Condense this down to keywords such as: (in) "I gain power," and (out) "I banish problems." As you think these words, try to feel that this is actually happening. Do not strain; simply relax and think about these beneficial ideas in the manner suggested. Keep this up for as long as you like.

Now relax your body by directing your attention away from your breathing and allowing yourself to breathe quite normally. Move your attention to your feet and, using the same idea of letting go, imagine that your feet are getting heavier and heavier. No need to strain, just imagine that this is so. Think to yourself, "My feet are getting heavier and heavier. They are lead. They sink downward, so I let go. I let them relax." Do this slowly and deliberately, until you feel that this is actually happening. Then say to yourself, "I let them go. I dismiss them from my mind, for they no longer concern me." The best way to proceed is to presume that this is actually happening, rather than concentrating on it or trying to force it to happen. In short, you pretend that this is happening and then dismiss the thought from your mind.

Now slowly move your attention to your legs and use the same idea of heaviness and eventual dismissal from your mind. Slowly work your way upward, through your body, completing the process by letting your face muscles, your forehead, and, finally, the top of your head relax completely.

Some of you may find this difficult at first. This is not unusual. In fact I would be surprised if anyone achieved any great depth of relaxation after only one or two attempts. Keep up the practice and you will soon master this new idea of letting go. In fact, practice as often as you like, for, not only is this a valuable prelude to real creative work, it is also guaranteed to reduce stress and improve your general health. So do not give up. Remind yourself of the benefits that creative visualization can bring and keep in mind that every new skill has to be learned and practiced. There are no shortcuts. When you are confident that you can relax (and this is all a question of personal judgment), move on to the next stage, in which we bring in the idea of creative thinking.

Affirmations

Creative thinking, as its name implies, is not like ordinary thought. It is rather special. Ordinary thinking has no effect on the inner mind, and for a very good reason. If every fleeting thought did indeed gain access to the inner mind, life would be just about impossible. Fortunately this cannot happen. There is a "screen" that filters out unimportant thoughts and prevents them from actually reaching the inner mind and thereby coming true. That "screen" blocks out conscious thoughts, and acts as a key that unlocks the doorways to the power of the inner mind. What is this safety-screen? It's the ability of your inner mind to judge the quality of your thoughts, so that only the right ones get through.

There are many methods that may be used to enlist the aid of the inner mind. One of these involves the use of affirmations. What exactly is an affirmation? It is the use of a repetitive phrase or desire designed to impact on subconscious levels. Repetition performed in the right way gets results. Let me illustrate this.

If you say or think to yourself, "I am healthy," nothing will happen, for it is simply a manufactured thought. It therefore carries no power. If you now say to yourself, "I *am* healthy," and mean it, there is a world of difference, because there is now intention tied to this thought. The inner mind will now become receptive to this idea. If you use the process known as affirmation—repeating the same statement, with conviction, over and over—the inner mind begins to respond to this. Repetition gets results if done with conviction and determination. You can see this effect in action when someone is learning a new skill, such as playing a musical instrument. The "learning" of the instrument is done through constant, repetitive practice. Once "learned," the skill becomes automatic, because your inner mind has stored this information in memory. No longer do you have to think about which note to play. You have "learned" it.

In order to make use of affirmations, you must first phrase your desire in an acceptable way and then repeat it deliberately, using a rhythm whenever possible. The best times are immediately after getting up in the morning, or just before drifting off to sleep at night. The affirmation should be repeated deliberately, with feeling. If you wish, you may gradually bring in the simultaneous use of the imagination, so that you also see your desire coming true. Do not rush this. Take your time and repeat the affirmation often. If you are musically inclined, you might like to turn this into a chant of sorts, so that it has a certain "ring" or lyricism to it. It is also a good idea to make this a self-discipline. In other words, make yourself chant this each day at specific times or use it in conjunction with a symbolic framework or power base. I will show you how later!

Affirmations can and do gain remarkable results. Furthermore there are no restrictions to their scope or coverage. For example, if you desire wealth, you might say: "With each passing day, I shall, like a magnet, attract more and more money into my life." If you desire health, you might say: "With the rising Sun of each day, so shall I draw into myself all of life's healing energies." It makes no difference whether you speak the affirmation aloud or silently within your mind. What does matter is that you have thought out your statement of intent carefully, saying the affirmation with conviction. If you do, you are bound to get results. It is a fact that one of the ways in which we "learn" is by repetition and, of course, we already know that the inner mind can learn many things. After all, you have learned how to read and write, how to add up numbers, and many other skills as well. Useful though these skills may be, however, they are purely mundane.

So where is all this leading? Have you ever heard statements like, "If you keep telling yourself that you are ill, you will eventually be ill"? Or perhaps, "He or she has convinced himself or herself that they cannot do this"? How do people convince themselves that a certain thing is true? Quite simply by repeating the idea over and over in their mind, to the exclusion of ideas to the contrary. The lesson here is that, if you can convince yourself that something bad is going to happen, you can just as easily convince yourself that the reverse is also possible.

Let me put this another way. Nothing ever advances in this world until someone convinces themselves that a certain idea is possible. To do this, they have to believe that this can be done, despite the supposed "facts" or what others may choose to think. They are convinced, and so they succeed. The rest, unfortunately, presumed that the reverse was true, and so, for them, it was. A great part of convincing yourself that something can be done, despite the odds, is to repeat the idea over and over in your mind until it is "learned" by your inner mind. Once this is done, the results are inevitable.

You can use this same idea to achieve any result. All you need is time to practice. Remember that the technique follows a pattern:

1. You must ignore the apparent "facts" or the "obvious," always bearing in mind that these things are only true because they are believed to be so. As you will see, the facts always respond to beliefs. Hence, it naturally follows that, if beliefs are changed, the supposed "fact" will also change. Before you begin to doubt this, at least try out the theory. There is a lot to be gained.

2. A calm mind makes for easier access to the inner mind. Before performing this excersise, relax and become peaceful. This technique is often used by athletes before an event. They calm down and then "psyche" themselves up by going over the event in their minds in a positive manner. In short, they attempt to convince themselves that they can win. What chance would they stand if they simply arrived in a nonchalant mood? The answer is, a very small one!

3. Choose a key phrase that sums up your intention, using the minimum number of words to get the maximum clarity. For instance, if your intention is to gain self-confidence, use a phrase such as, "With each passing day, I *will* become more confident." Note the emphasis on the word "will." This is most important. All phrases must be positive and assertive if they are to be fully effective.

4. Having chosen your phrase, relax fully and then repeat it, in your mind, slowly and deliberately, for a few minutes. The

amount of time devoted to this is entirely up to you—there are no hard and fast rules. Do not simply repeat the words, however. Put some feeling into it. Mean what you say. The more sincere you are, the better the result.

The art of affirmations is extremely effective if carried out with conviction and persistence. Furthermore, it can be used for any desire or intention that you have in mind. First, think about what you want. Turn this over in your mind, so that it is clear and understood. Then choose a suitable phrase to sum up your desire and, using the procedure given, repeat your affirmation in a positive and assertive manner on a regular basis, say, once or twice each day. The best times to do this are early morning or late at night before you fall asleep. The latter time is most effective, especially if you go through the relaxation exercise while lying in bed and then repeat your affirmation just before going to sleep. It does not matter if you drift into sleep while doing this. In fact, this actually helps the affirmation to have a greater effect because there is less resistance from the conscious mind.

Affirmations are extremely useful and can be valuable tools in the practice of creative visualization. With practice, they are very effective and, once the procedure is learned, they can be used at any time—while you are out walking, or at any spare moment you may have. Affirmations not only help to make constructive use of your spare time, they also get results.

Chapter 6

Creative Visualization

The future is not set in tablets of stone. Through creative visualization, with its visions of success, you hold the key to achieving that which you most desire. Creative visualization is a relatively simply technique that requires practice and perseverance. If you are prepared to make the commitment, however, you can achieve a prosperous and happy new life.

We turn now to the most powerful tool you possess—your imagination. Your imagination is not only powerful, it is easy to use. If I ask you to describe a daffodil without you actually looking at one, a picture of this flower arises in your mind. You see the flower in your imagination. The more you think about it, the more clearly you see the flower. Some of you will have no difficulty in sustaining this picture, others will only catch a fleeting glance, but you will all be able to see it. The image of the daffodil is firmly fixed in your memory—in other words, in your inner mind. Try this with other objects, such as your car, your home, or even a friend. The same process takes place. When you think about something, your memory gives you a picture of it. Moreover, the more you relax and keep your mind on a subject, the more "involved" you become and the more vivid the pictures become.

Using your imagination for creative work simply extends your natural ability to see pictures in your own mind. Anyone can see mental pictures. In fact, you have all indulged in daydreaming, which is an uncontrolled form of using your imagination. Creative visualization is all about controlling your imagination. In fact, you can turn daydreaming into a powerful tool for self-enhancement. In a daydream, your mind wanders from one subject to another in a random pattern; there is no control. Worrying or brooding over problems is simply a more potent form of the act of imagining. Look at what happens when you worry. Mental pictures are generated. Unlike the example of the daffodil, these images don't necessarily arise from your memory—they are manufactured by your mind. Thus, the imagination is not limited to memory alone. Pictures can, and are, produced by the mind that represent events that have not yet happened. This fact is made use of in creative visualization.

When you worry or brood, the pictures your mind invents are not true. They are invented, or merely presumed to be true, based on apparent "facts." The danger is that those pictures can *become* true, because the inner mind responds to the imagination. In short, negative images can quite easily become fact. Fortunately, the reverse is also true. Daydreaming, and to a certain extent imagined difficulties, are largely ignored by the inner mind due to the same safety mechanism that filters out everyday, fleeting thoughts. The deliberate use of the imagination, however, is not ignored. Imaginative images will be acted on if they are sustained.

You experienced no difficulty in seeing the daffodil in your imagination. And if I ask you to imagine $1000 in bundles of notes, you probably won't have too much difficulty with this either. Try it for yourself. The difference with this image is that it does not arise from memory. You construct it deliberately. So far, it is simply a picture in your imagination. It will not influence the inner mind, because it is not an instruction. To change the image to an instruction, you must simply change your thinking. With the daffodil, the intention in generating the image was to describe the flower. With the $1000, you oriented your thinking around an idea of this amount of money. To actually acquire $1000, the inner mind must be given the image in a specific way so that it can act on it and cause it to become real. Using the imagination in this way is known as creative visualization. We will examine this in detail and explore ways to activate your reality-shaping mechanism, using the right triggers. These triggers have the potential of becoming commands to empower your inner mind to realize that which you most desire. This process uses three aspects of your mind: the power of thought, the power of feeling, and the power of the imagination.

The first stage in this process is to create an intention. In other words, you must know exactly what you want. You must therefore think about your intention carefully and come to a decision. One of the greatest causes of failure in creative visualization is that people really do not know what they want. If this is true, how on Earth can their inner mind be expected to realize their desires? Muddled or inconclusive thinking produces erratic results—if it produces any results at all. While creating your intention, it is important that you not allow yourself to be swayed by apparent facts or difficulties. Your inner mind only recognizes difficulties and obstacles if you tell it that these exist, otherwise it will ignore them. Always bear in mind that the only real limitations are those that you place on yourself by accepting, or believing, that these can prevent success. Keep all your thinking positive and you are bound to get positive results.

By deciding on an intention, you opened a channel along which your inner mind can function on your behalf. The next stage is to hold to that thought regardless of circumstances. Be persistent in presenting this desire to your inner mind. This may be done by using affirmations, as suggested. In addition, never let negative thoughts get in the way. You will find that doubts and uncertainties creep into your mind from time to time. Each time they do, push them to one side, realize that they are not true unless you allow them to become so, and then reaffirm your intention. It helps if you keep in mind that the results must come if you are persistent and that, as you change your thinking, so you are bound to change your circumstances. The more positively you think about your desire, the quicker the result will be. The actual time that this may take to materialize is difficult to specify, as there are many factors involved. The important thing to remember is that to persist is to succeed.

To ensure success and speed up results, you can bring your imagination into play through creative visualization. This is done by constructing a picture in your mind of the very thing that you are trying to achieve. This is not difficult. All you have to do is to think deliberately about what you want and your imagination will supply the images. It helps if you are relaxed and have spent some time using an affirmation to focus your mind on the desire. It is, however, very important that you be positive in the use of your imagination and that you use it in such a way that your inner mind will accept its images as an instruction rather than a daydream. One of the best ways to ensure that this occurs is to use creative visualization. This is easy to do. Since your intention is to actually *have* the thing you desire, all you have to do is imagine that this is so—that you actually do have the very thing you desire. Suppose that you actually wish for that $1000. First think about this sum of money. You might see it as several piles of notes or even as a check. Try not to be rigid or force the imagination. Allow it to work and give it lots of scope. To move from this imaginative act to creative visualization, simply think about actually having the $1000, but think about it as though it were true. Pretend that this is true and, in your imagination, see yourself actually having the money, holding it, and even spending it. Indulge yourself in this vision for as long as you like and put some feeling into it. After all, if you really did suddenly have $1000, how would you feel? Elated, to say the least!

This is not a child's game or some flight of fancy. It is a scientific way of ensuring that you get the cooperation of your inner mind. How? By exploiting the simple fact that your inner mind does not know the difference between what you see (and therefore believe to be true) and what you imagine to be true. A very useful fact! The persistent use of creative visualization is thus scientific, and can be proven to get results when all else fails. It is well worthy of consideration, even if it does take a little practice. In any case, what is the alternative? Giving up and allowing opportunity to pass you by?

Creative visualization is the first step along the road to re-instating the principle that the acausal connection of events at the macrocosmic level can be effected by the use of reality-shaping techniques on the microcosmic level. In other words, although it is easier to bring about small changes in the cosmos than it is to effect huge ones, an accumulation of microcosmic changes will generate macrocosmic change over time. The key is in knowing where and when to make those small changes. It is easier to influence a situation that is still "embryonic," or better yet, one that has not even begun to happen, than it is to influence it at a later time. Creative visualization maintains that, once a formulated visualized intention has set up an initial set of conditions through persistent use, it will indeed happen, given time. This gives you the power to control the material side of your life. This is important, for there can never be any real understanding of the mysteries of life until this first step is mastered. Look at life, then have the courage to change things by the persistent use of creative visualization and affirmations. In particular, look at yourself, at the way you react to life, at your habits, and at your general approach to problems. Be honest. Are you positive or negative? The more positive you are, the better your life will be and the more control you will gain.

Through conditioning, you have been led to believe that most things are impossible. They are not. Remember, however, that everything takes time. There is no such thing as "instant" success. This is why you must persist, refusing to give way to what seems to be the obvious. Never give up or abandon your desire without a very good reason. The only real reason for giving up is if your desire may be harmful, either to yourself or to someone else. How will you know if an intention is potentially harmful? Your inner mind will inevitably bring this to your attention, for it seeks to serve only your best interests. Consequently, if something is wrong or there is a better way of achieving success, your inner mind will seek to bring this to your attention. But until you have a good reason, persist and resolve to win.

With time and practice, you will learn to eliminate negative thinking and brush apparent problems aside. The responsibility for this rests solely with you, for, although you may learn from others, it is *your* mind and *your* life. You must make the effort. You must train your mind in the same way that athletes train their bodies to respond, or a musician masters an instrument. All these skills involve a gradual process of improvement and expansion of natural abilities. No athlete could ever hope to break a world record without a lot of dedication and effort. This is the very thing that sets a record-breaker apart from the others. More practice, more dedication, more enthusiasm—better results. Behind all this lies the power of belief, for those who do believe are bound to succeed when others fail. This is the real difference between an ordinary person and a champion. The latter is motivated by positive beliefs and has the ability to see beyond present limits. Your mind needs training, not by strenuous workouts, but by firm, persistent control and by re-education to the real facts of life, some of which are given in this book. By doing this, you will discover the power of the mind for, like a trained muscle, it can do far more when it is exercised than when it is simply left to stagnate.

Image Control

If you accept the multidimensional paradigm of space/time in which Einsteinian physics and quantum theory fuse to give the picture of a cosmos in which, if anything can happen, it ultimately does, then you need to be more in control of your mental imagery. If the car that missed hitting you on your way to work did hit you in a different reality, or the lottery number that never came up has, somewhere and somehow, made you wealthy beyond your wildest dreams, then you must train your visualizing faculty to help you choose your most positive reality. Once your visualizing ability has reached a satisfactory level, the technique should be put into practice to ensure that you maximize your physical reality. Clearly, in the examples given above, your inner mind should work toward that reality in which you avoid being hit by the car and collect on the lottery ticket!

For anyone interested in seeing whether a little practice in visualization can make a difference, I offer the following exercises. This is a good way to learn how to visualize, especially if you are a concrete thinker who has trouble imagining things. Holding a steady picture or image in your mind may be difficult for you. All manner of distractions may creep in. But visualization, or the ability to imagine with intent, means being able to hold a reasonably clear picture in your mind's eye.

To practice, put some objects in front of you and relax. The objects can be anything: a bottle, a cup, a ring, an ornament. Now fix your eyes on one object and try to remember everything about it, the color and shape. Then "close" your eyes and try to visualize the object. If it disappears, try to recall it. In the beginning, you may only be able to do this for a few seconds. As time goes by, however, and with regular practice, the length of time you can hold the visualized image will actually increase until you can visualize whatever you like and hold it for as long as you like. The purpose of the exercise will be achieved when you can hold one object in your mind's eye without any interruption for about two minutes.

When you reach this point, you may start to imagine the objects with your eyes "open." Again, visualize one object without interruption for about two minutes. When you reach this stage, you will know that you can visualize properly, if you go about it the right way. All you have to do is look at what you want to visualize long enough to get it fixed in your memory.[1]

---

[1]Alternatively, you can use the four tattva symbols and the methods outlined in Ophiel's book to develop this faculty in yourself. See *The Art and Practice of Getting Material Things Through Creative Visualization*, by Ophiel (York Beach, ME: Samuel Weiser, 1975).

Chapter 7

Symbolism

The difference between "mind power" and magic is that the former is only part of the picture, a small, albeit important, branch of the larger science of Magick. Magick is the whole science. It offers an additional dimension that is often missed, yet one that is capable of great things. That extra dimension is known as symbolism.

What is symbolism? When C. G. Jung discusses symbols, he contends that "thus a word or image is symbolic when it implies something more than its obvious and immediate meaning."[1] The inner mind deals with three kinds of symbols. First, there are abstract symbols, such as the pentagram, the hexagram, the circle, triangle, or square. There are also personified symbols that usually take a humanoid shape, like gods, demons, and angels. These symbols epitomize a type of power, and their construction is known as the art of telesmatic images. These arose when individuals constructed specific, personal images to represent a definite type of energy, thereby forging a link to powers which would otherwise be difficult to access. Much depends on the individual and their needs in this process. The exact type of image produced depends on the person projecting the image. No two people are alike. Nor will they have the same viewpoint concerning energy and its use.

The third type of symbol that can instruct the inner mind is pure geographical imagery: thinking about something in the

---

[1] C. G. Jung, et al. *Man and His Symbols* (London: Aldus Books, 1964; London: MacMillan, 1978), p. 4.

imagination—pictures. These symbols are powerful, not because they come from the gods, but for the simple reason that they represent a language of power, a language that the inner mind fully understands. Symbols are the keys that unlock the doors to power—if they are used correctly.

C. G. Jung regarded unconscious processes as belonging to two systems. The conscious aspect of the psyche, he taught, can be likened to that part of an island we can see above water. But there is an infinitely larger part of that island below the water, a part that we cannot see. This represents the unconscious. There may also be a part of the island that was not always covered by the sea, and it may well be possible to reclaim this part. This represents what Jung calls the personal unconscious. The part of the island that was always covered by the sea represents the collective unconscious. The ego—the conscious, thinking part of the mind—is but a very small part of the total psyche.

The collective unconscious of Jungian psychology correlates with the astral level of esoteric teaching. This is a vast reserve of tendencies formed from experiences rooted in the remote past of the human race. Jung called these tendencies archetypes. They emerge as imagery and symbols in dreams and also occur in the mythos and mythology of all culture and races.

These primordial images of the collective unconscious exercise a potent influence on our lives. This influence is often completely misunderstood, because it is unknown to the conscious mind. Speech is a comparatively recent evolutionary development and these unconcious levels of the mind predate it, their origins lying in the race's primitive past. Thus the only way to communicate with the unconscious mind (inner mind) is through symbols.

"Symbolism is a vital and easy means of expressing subconscious knowledge, vision or sensation that is difficult or impossible to express simply in a few words," says A. O. Spare.

"Symbolism in its nature, is either arbitrary or true representation reduced to pictorial simplicity, analogous when of an abstract."[2]

To understand what a symbol is, consider the number "1." It is a symbol, though you may not think so. This simple character conveys quite a lot of information, all of which is condensed into the familiar symbol "1." For instance, when you see a statement such as "1 egg," it means *one* egg, not two, or none at all—it means a single egg. The symbol "1" therefore gives precise information and defines exact limits. Another example is that of a musical note. Depending on its shape and position on the stave, it conveys precise information to the musician as to the pitch and duration of the note. This information can only be understood by our conscious minds, however, if they have been educated to do so. For instance, the musical note just mentioned would mean nothing to a nonmusician. It (the symbol) is constant and contains very specific information. Our ability to understand and therefore use this information, is dependent on training.

Look at any road sign. It is a symbol and, as such, it conveys a host of information to travelers in a very concise form—far more quickly, in fact, than would be possible with words. This condensed information can be seen by drivers and acted on without their having to think. This is the real value of a symbol—its ability to bypass the normal, and slower, conscious mind. The advantages of man-made symbols are quite obvious. For instance, what is preferable when approaching a crossroads: a large sign explaining that, before you may proceed, you must stop and look both ways, or a black cross on a white background? The symbol (see figure 1, page 62) is far easier to see and interpret and is, incidentally, far safer.

---

[2]Austin Osman Spare, *The Book of Pleasure (Self Love). The Psychology of Ecstasy* (Northampton, England: Sut Anubis, 1987), p. 52.

Figure 1. The road sign.

Man-made symbols quickly convey large amounts of information without having to use the much slower verbal method. In much the same way, creative symbols convey information to the inner mind. These, like the man-made symbols, have to be studied and worked with if they are to have any real worth. Moreover, it is vital that these symbols be worked with in the right way, free from religious overtones or other encumbrances.

Chapter 8

Centering and
Cleansing the Ritual Space

This centering exercise is suitable for counteracting feelings of impurity (especially prior to erecting the cosmic sphere, a process fully explained in the next chapter). It can also act to dispel psychic debris from the area in which your creative visualization is to take place.

Take a few minutes to quiet your mind. Feel and visualize either a brilliant, pearly lunar sphere or an incandescent solar disk glowing and shining above your head. As you breathe in, begin to draw the Sun-Moon down. It will pass slowly, very slowly, through your body with each inhalation, filling you with a pure, clean radiance. When it has passed completely through your body and into the floor, reverse the process and raise the light disk up through your body, this time synchronized with each exhalation (this is optional), until it shines once more above your head (see figure 2, page 64).

You may pay particular attention to any part of the body that needs healing or cleansing. Be especially thorough whenever you feel tired, stressed, or drained. Suitable background music, together with some appropriate incense, can aid this exercise enormously. This exercise can be performed as a prelude and as an ending to the cosmic sphere exercise.

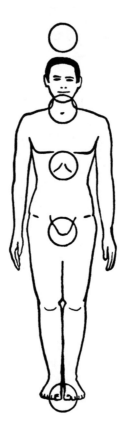

Figure 2. The lunar sphere/solar disk centering ritual.

Chapter 9

Circles of Power

The following exercise is important for two reasons: it helps you to relax and push away distracting thoughts, and it serves as a potent symbol that your inner mind fully understands. With patient practice, this exercise is guaranteed to bring a response from your inner mind that may not be possible by any other means. All you have to do is manipulate your consciousness so that you create what you wish, rather than what you have been given. Symbols, as you now know, are the language of the inner mind. By using the master symbol of the circle of power, you communicate directly with this powerful part of yourself. This symbol acts as an "on/off switch" for power.

This exercise should be treated seriously, even though it may not appear to be particularly "sensational" or astounding. The secret of true creative visualization, or reality-shaping, lies in the use of simple yet natural principles. The truth is simple, and so is the way to power. In the words of a great man, who left clues to this: "Verily I say unto you, whosoever shall not receive the kingdom of God as a little child, he shall not enter therein" (Mark 10:15). The truth is simple to a child, before society forces it into a mold. For adults, the truth is often more difficult to perceive, because of the conditioned belief that life is "complex."

As with all effective creative visualization, you must start this exercise by relaxing in surroundings that are conducive to concentration. This exercise may be done seated; your eyes may be open or closed. What you are about to do is to build a cosmic sphere in your imagination, in which you will later perform creative visualization with far greater effect. This sphere is sometimes known as the "cosmic in-world." Physicality is an extension of this imaginary condition. Your place of work serves only to remind you of the real inner world within your own mind. It is also a workroom from which you may exclude the outside world and where you can work undisturbed in congenial surroundings.

Symbols are the keys that unlock the doorways to power and so it is to symbolism that we must turn if we are to discover a realistic base plan leading to success.

The Master Symbol

The master symbol is an encircled cross (see figure 3, below). Like the circuit diagram of the electronic engineer, this symbol is a plan of power to those who know how to use it. We will examine this symbol in some detail in order to see how this works.

The Center

The central point of the circle represents the power of your inner mind. It is that part of you which mediates power and is connected to everything that exists or has existed. The power

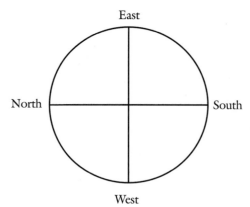

Figure 3.
The encircled cross.

of the center is *yours*. It is not distant, nor is it difficult to contact. Treat your central inner-mind power realistically by adopting positive and essentially beneficial beliefs. By doing this, you open up the channels of power, rather than blocking them with unfounded beliefs.

The Cross

The cross is a symbol of power in action, flowing outward from the center along the four paths that make up the arms of the cross. A reasonable comparison would be to the wires or printed circuits that connect electronic components and allow electricity to flow. Each path is "ruled" by an element—air, fire, water, and earth. In modern times, these four vertices can be seen to represent space, time, mass, and energy, or the four fundamental forces that govern the nature of the cosmos: electromagnetism, strong nuclear force, weak nuclear force, and gravity. They give the cosmos its basic form. If you take way any one of them or alter their qualities, even slightly, you create a completely different universe. Without electromagnetism, there would be no chemistry or biology, nor would there be heat from the Sun. Take away the strong nuclear force and there would be no nuclei—it could not exist. There would be no atoms or molecules; the Sun and stars would be unable to generate heat and light from nuclear energy. Do away with the weak nuclear force and vital, life-giving heavy elements would not be able to come into existence. Eliminate gravity and there would be no galaxies, stars, or planets. The universe would not and could not exist.

The four elements bear little resemblance to their physical counterparts and should be considered more as four different ways of expressing power. There is no need for us to discuss the complexities of these elements. It is sufficient to recognize that these do exist, albeit on a symbolic level, allowing the inner mind to work through these four channels. In short, if we make

provision for power to flow through its natural elemental channels, the inner mind will respond. And it will do this far better
than if we ignore the elements altogether.

The Circle

As the central point of the circle represents the beginning, so
the circle itself represents the end and completion. Everything created by the center is contained within the circle. All
through life, we form circles, to a greater or lesser degree.
You can see this quite easily if you look around. Circles link
together and, at the same time, they exclude anything that
falls outside their central theme. All kinds of circles, from
close friendships to secret societies, exhibit these tendencies.
Circles, therefore, both *encompass* and *exclude*. This principle
is used in creative visualization, which has the potential of
making a mockery of physical science by giving direct access
to the mind in order to activate a reality-shaping mechanism.
The inner mind fully understands the inner truth of the circle. Thus we can use this symbolism to get full inner-mind
cooperation.

The encircled cross forms a fitting power base for many
reasons. The inner mind recognizes this fact and responds to
it. But this symbol also contains many mysteries within its
simple design that make it an admirable subject for meditation. We will limit our discussion, however, to the more
pragmatic issue of using this symbol within the context of
ritual.[1]

---

[1]Every church ceremony contains a certain degree of ritual. The opening of a
daily session in school begins with a ritual that may consist simply of singing
a few songs and repeating the pledge of allegiance to the nation's flag. A the-
atrical performance begins with the ritual of having the orchestra play an
opening number, perhaps the national anthem. Ritualism is merely a formal
process whereby we start to do certain definite things. It may pertain to material acts, or to mental acts. We may say that ritual is the customary enact-
ment or dramatization of an idea.

The Cosmic Sphere

Although the encircled cross is a flat image, it is still quite valuable. Since we live in a three-dimensional world however, we must construct from it a three-dimensional symbolic power base for creative visualization. This leads us to the concept of the cosmic *sphere*, rather than a plain circle. Do not be put off by the apparent complexity of the following procedure. It is really quite simple to follow with a little patient practice, and the results are well worth the additional effort, as you will see. Figure 4 will help you visualize the cosmic sphere.

The construction of a cosmic sphere starts at the central point, from which radiate six paths joined by three concentric circles known as the triple rings. To ritualize its construction is quite simple. It is accomplished by using opening and closing formulas to bracket the process. The validity of this opening and closing structure will prove itself with regular practice. It is particularly important to remember that you are working within your imagination, using an imaginary "instate." In the beginning, you should practice the cosmic sphere in a standing

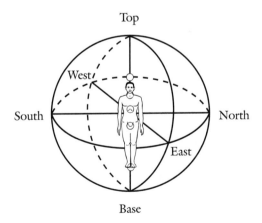

Figure 4. The cosmic sphere.

position. After having acquired sufficient experience, you may try other positions as well.

Creative Visualization— Opening Formula

Start, as always, by relaxing and clearing your mind of all mundane thoughts. Before you undertake any creative visualization work you should go through a period of preliminary meditation. This can be done by using the lunar/solar centering ritual as a prelude and ending (see page 63).

Time is relative and is created entirely by ourselves. So, in a temporal sense, the lunar/solar centering ritual can lead you smoothly from real time into dream time. At this point, imagine a point of bright light inside yourself, at about heart level. See a shaft of light rise upward to some convenient distance (6 to 8 feet), thereby forming the first path. Do the same in a downward direction to form the second path. After practicing for a while, you will notice that the light actually flows simultaneously in both directions. The beam is a continuous current, not a quick flash. Feel this energy streaming through you. This is often experienced as a warm, tingling sensation, or as a feeling of strength and power. You can visualize this beam as a white, translucent color.

Now form the arms of the cross by imagining a beam of light proceeding from center toward an imaginary east which, of course, lies in front of you. (The beam should travel about the same distance as before—6 to 8 feet.) Feel this energy streaming through you. Repeat this to an imaginary south (your right), an imaginary west (behind you), and finally toward an imaginary north (your left).

All that remains is to complete the sphere by adding the triple rings of the cosmos. The first ring starts from the uppermost point. You can imagine this as a ring of light proceeding in a clockwise direction through south, base, north, and finally returning to the top. The second ring also starts at the top, but this time, it moves forward through east, base, west, and back to the top. The third and middle ring forms the inner center. Its function is close to that of the magical circle. With it, you focus your power and move into the center of your own inner universe. (Remember that, according to Einstein, everywhere is the center of the universe.) This third ring starts at east and proceeds in a clockwise direction through south, west, north, and back to east.

The cosmic sphere is now complete. This is your inner space, without which you would have no background against which to view the manifestations of your inner mind.

Creative Visualization— Closing Formula

To close down the cosmic sphere, simply reverse the procedure, finally seeing the central light inside yourself disappear. Remember that it is not important that you hold a vivid picture of this in your mind or strain to see it. Follow the guidance given on the use of the imagination in the creative visualization chapter. Relax and imagine that the sphere is being constructed around you. Your inner mind will understand what you are doing, because you are thinking creatively. Children, who have the gift of imagination, have little or no difficulty living in "other" worlds. They know how to pretend. There is nothing wrong with pretending, if it is done constructively. So pretend that you are constructing the cosmic sphere and let go of the restrictions that tell you that this is silly. I assure you that it is not. In fact, you will find this technique advocated in many "mind-power" books, in which you are advised to act and think as though you actually *have* the thing you desire. This may be sound psychology, but is it not also pretense in a positive form? By practicing and then using this symbol pattern of the cosmic sphere, you have prepared the way for this pretense to have a far more potent effect. You have found fertile ground in which to plant the seeds of desire.

This practical symbol pattern can be carried around in your imagination. Furthermore it can be used anywhere, because all you have to do is construct it and then, in your imagination, start to think creatively. If you do, all manner of things start to get quickly done. It has lots of everyday uses. I have known it to do lots of things for me, and for other people. Some have reported such odd things as obtaining a parking space when there were none and seeing bank managers when there was no chance. My favorite story is of a dear old lady who was suffering terrible pain in the shoulder that would not respond to normal medical treatment. She sat down, erected the cosmic sphere, and worked for healing in her imagination (within the cosmic sphere structure), and, within ten minutes, the pain disappeared. It has not been back since. This is the sort of thing that can be done.

The cosmic sphere, as is already apparent from its description, can also serve as psychic protection, for opening and closing, and as an energy charge, especially before and after stressful, powerful creative visualization sessions.

Chapter 10

A Paradigm
for Creative Visualization

The technique of creative visualization is not new. There has never been a time when it didn't form the very basis of magical training. Most of the so-called popular psychology books utilize it without going into details about the principles involved.

Creative visualization, with its version of an alternative reality, works on a biofeedback paradigm. What you visualize as your desire actually acts upon you as a subconscious motivator, guiding your steps along the future path you envision!

Creative visualization is a particular art used by magicians. Through it, they perform nearly all their seeming miracles. Through it, the world's greatest powers become your coworkers. It is a great help in all affairs of life, and it is also a help in maintaining health, attaining success, wealth, and love, and creating happiness. Here is a model that should be followed every time you need to visualize, no matter for what purpose. I warn you, however, that there is an apparent anomaly in these guidelines in relation to some others that I will give you later on in this book.

1. The visualized desire must refer to only one subject, one thing, one cause, one result, or one intention. You must focus your creative powers, just as the light coming through a magnifying glass is focused on a single point on a single object. You cannot combine several desires or several purposes, in

one act of visualization.[1] That is one of the most serious mistakes that a person can make. They believe that, as long as they are about to devote a half-hour to silent visualization, they might as well combine several purposes and save time. But this very combination of thoughts prevents concentration. There must be only one thought in the mind during visualization.

2. If you followed the advice given by most writers on the subject of creative visualization, you would be so busy concentrating on the rules of visualization that you'd never get anywhere. This concentration itself would cause an internal dialogue, so there would be little concentration on anything else. So I say to anybody embarking on this sort of work that the best method is the *least* method. One principle of visualization holds that the more you think of what you are trying to do with your inner mind, the more you interfere with the process that makes the result possible. In other words, the more you are objectively aware of the plans and details of visualization, the less chance you have of getting the instruction to the inner mind. This is called attunement.

3. The proper way to achieve attunement is to *stop* your objective thinking, and that is the hardest thing for the beginner to do. Have you ever tried to stop thinking? Chances are that, after you try for half a second, you will begin to wonder whether you have stopped thinking. Your mind will become analytical, you will begin to wonder whether you are succeeding, and so forth. All this amounts to interference. It must end before you can achieve proper attunement. You must cease to know who you are, where you are, why you

---

[1]Multipurpose intentions can be attempted when you have gained experience and success with single objectives. Their failure is usually due to the inherent problem of negative thinking and lack of persistence. Surface thinking, presumption, or a vague hope simply will not do. Your mind is a powerful tool. In order to use it to maximum effect, it has to be "programmed" correctly.

are, or even *that* you are at all. You must lose conscious knowledge of your own existence. You must have only one simple thought, and that must be the single thought of what you are visualizing.

4. After you have read this chapter, forget the rules and follow your own inclinations, remembering that thinking of rules and laws will prevent your success. As soon as you have decided on a single intention, center and erect the cosmic sphere, described in previous chapters. Then sit down where it is quiet. When you have reached a satisfactory state of calm, light a white candle that symbolizes inner peace and the eternal source of power. Symbolism is very important in creative visualization, for symbols and symbolic acts such as this speak volumes to your inner mind. Now gaze upon the lighted candle, using it as a focusing aid (more on this later). After some practice, you will be able to concentrate in the dark or in daylight, without anything to gaze at. Sitting in silence, draw a mental picture of the thing you wish to have result from the visualization. In other words, visualize clearly what you want, then stop thinking of it.

In making your mental picture, imagine that you are an artist about to draw upon a white canvas the thing you wish, either literally or symbolically. Have the picture develop slowly on the canvas of the mind and in truth. See it! Make it as real as you can. Then *stop!* There is a danger line. It is so hard to stop, but you must stop so that the objective mind can release the picture. It cannot do that as long as you keep working on the picture. Close your eyes and *think of nothing*, not even of yourself, the person who is to be benefited, the cosmos, the world, the room, or anything else. As you stop thinking and dismiss all thoughts from your mind, do so with the feeling that "all is well and your desires will be fulfilled." When you are finished, close down the cosmic sphere and center.

It will take practice to get into the habit of visualizing in this way. You must overcome the habit of dwelling too long on the desire you are visualizing. Look at the candle just long enough to picture in your mind that which you want to see in the candlelight. Then stop thinking about it and gaze at the candle with a blank look, without analyzing or questioning. Gradually, you will become aware of a response. If you wish news from a friend, health, love, a favor, or anything else, visualize it and dismiss it from your mind. Sit without thinking for a while—preferably for about three minutes, but even one minute will do for the mind to communicate your desire, your symbol picture, to the inner mind. Then rise from your visualizing with no further thought on the matter. Rest in the confidence that it will be done. To have doubts or be skeptical during your visualizing or after it means sending those doubts to the inner mind—doubts that what you desire will come to you. And this doubt interferes with a positive response.

Part
Three

Perfecting the Art

Chapter 11

The Way to Recovery

As you have read, it is your inner mind that influences life, mainly through your existing beliefs and dominant thoughts. Creative visualization is the science of understanding and using the vast potential of the inner mind. It is the "inner mind" that mediates power on your behalf and, as a result, influences circumstances. How is this done? Without entering into a complete discussion on the workings of the inner mind, I will give a brief explanation. Those who wish to dig a little deeper may do so by using various magical techniques given in my other books.[1]

In brief, there is an abundant supply of life energy. It is without limit and without end. Here on Earth, everything which exists contains some of this energy. Far from there being only one energy pattern, there are an incalculable number of different types. The easiest way to understand this energy is to compare it with white light, which can be split up into the familiar colors of the spectrum. In the same way that it is possible to mix colors to produce thousands of shades, so it is with life energy. The permutations of the energy spectrum are endless. Each permutation will, of course, affect matter in a different way. As a result, that matter will be "colored" accordingly. The net result is the profusion of plants, flowers, trees, rocks, and metals so evident in nature. The inner mind knows every possible combination of the energy

---

[1]Phillip Cooper, *The Magickian: A Study in Effective Magick* (York Beach, ME: Samuel Weiser, 1993) and *Basic Magick: A Practical Guide* (York Beach, ME: Samuel Weiser, 1996).

patterns that make things "live." Like a vast computer, the inner mind can "tune in" to these combinations and make them respond to it, thus affecting their makeup. As the inner mind takes in an instruction, usually in the form of a belief, it seeks to influence everything that is likely to facilitate its quest to carry out this instruction. It does this easily. In fact, we can assume that the inner mind knows no limits and can achieve whatever it is instructed to do.

Any limits to which the inner mind is subjected are given to it in the form of beliefs. In short, if you believe that something is not possible, the inner mind will accept this. It will remain until a new instrucion is given. Try to move a solid object using only your mind. Chances are that you cannot. It is "impossible." Yet this has been done quite successfully by some people, simply because they knew it *was* possible. This is why it is so essential to question your existing beliefs. If you believe something to be difficult, out of reach, or completely impossible, then, for you, it is. You have defined the limits and believed them to be true. Your inner mind, with its need to serve, simply acts on this belief.

Creative visualization is the art of giving instructions to the inner mind in such a way that they will be accepted. Once accepted, they become fact. This may been done in many ways. Ritual is (or should be) the epitome of good technique, but not everyone wishes to become involved in the training in and understanding of cosmic laws, correspondences, and other matters so essential to this procedure. Other methods include hypnosis, alpha-state, affirmations, and the pure power of belief itself. In the initial stages, it is far better to keep things simple and to tread well-worn paths. Here are suggestions and ideas that, if followed, can ensure success without heavy cost in time or materials.

If I simply ask you to believe that tomorrow you will be very rich, you might find this exceedingly difficult, if not impossible. Why? For the simple reason that, under the present circumstances, it is obvious that this cannot be—in other words, it appears to be impossible. But what is the "obvious" other than a manifestation of beliefs? Facts depend on thoughts. The first rule of creative visualization is:

Learn to ignore the obvious
and
never accept the impossible as fact.

Why? If you have understood what has already been discussed, you will know the answer.

The inner mind always seeks to manifest what you believe to be true. What appears to be true, or "obvious," exists only as a result of your beliefs. Change those beliefs, and the "obvious" changes to accommodate them. The obvious, therefore, should not be accepted as absolute or unchangeable. It is therefore a serious mistake to assume that circumstances are unalterable. This kind of thinking, although popular among rationalists, is completely erroneous. The world may tell you that "what is done, is done" or that "seeing is believing." I am here to tell you that the people who believe this are narrowminded and that those who teach it are fools. What you see with your eyes is not necessarily true. Any hypnotist can prove this by making someone see something that does not exist. From another point of view, how do you know that the color you see as red, is red. Have you any proof? No, of course you have not. The only "proof" you have is that you were led to believe that a particular color is red. Nor can the rationalists explain why solid objects can be moved by pure thought, why certain people can walk on fire without being burned, why people can be cured of terminal illness when medical science gives up. No they cannot, nor will they be able to explain these "impossible" things until they realize the truth of the power of the mind and the fruitlessness of trying to analyze effects rather than causes.

To apply this principle is, at first, difficult. With steady practice, however, it soon becomes a habit. Forming new habits to replace old ones is also part of the art of creative visualization. Who needs bad habits, especially when they are causing harm? Do you? No, of course not. You must, therefore, resolve to master this next exercise until it becomes part of your everyday thinking and your life.

How do you start your day? By worrying over bills, racking your brains for ways to get more money, or indulging in depression? This is your first mistake—and possibly your worst one. What happens while you are doing this? You start to think and, as a result, you paint a rather gloomy picture in your mind. "Pictures" in the mind are very powerful. By thinking and creating mental pictures, you give instructions to your inner mind. Remember, in earlier chapters, when I said that the only way to get the inner mind to respond is to speak to it in a language that it can understand? Well, as I have already said the inner mind responds to mental pictures—symbols. You may have read about "visualization." There is a great deal of value in this technique, although the process itself is often difficult to master, due to a lack of basic information. To visualize simply means to see something in your mind. Daydreams are one example of this, albeit a nonproductive one. There seems to be a mistaken impression that, in order to use mental pictures correctly, you must see things vividly. This is not strictly true. Much depends on the individual. Some people can see imaginary pictures with ease, others cannot. It is not necessary to hold vivid pictures in your mind. What is necessary is that you think in a specific way, because the quality of your thinking determines whether or not those thoughts go through to the inner mind. Let me explain.

If I ask you to imagine that you are very rich and to hold a steady picture of this in your mind, you may have considerable difficulty doing so. All manner of distractions creep in, including worries, and, because there seems to be no point to the exercise, it soon deteriorates into a shambles. Certain elements essential to success are missing.

The Correct Procedure

The inner mind is more receptive when you are calm and relaxed. Tension, agitation, restlessness, and negative thoughts such as worry will all get in the way. The first rule is always to seek peace and tranquillity before you begin. Learn how to relax. Like everything else, this requires practice and some degree of patience. Persist and you will soon learn how to do this.

Relaxation is simply a process of letting go. First, find somewhere quiet, adopt a comfortable position, either sitting or lying down, then start to breathe slowly and easily. Take deep breaths, but do not strain. Keep in mind the idea of slowing down. After a while, direct your attention to your feet and imagine that they are getting heavier and heavier, then dismiss them as though they no longer existed. Keep in mind the idea of letting go. Let them relax, then let them simply fade from your mind. Don't try to force them out of your consciousness. Work your way slowly and gently through your body, right up to the top of your head. With practice, you will find this becomes easy.

The next stage, that of relaxing the mind itself, is often the biggest stumbling block to success. Until now, this has not been a problem, provided that you have entered into the spirit of the exercise, because your mind has been occupied with the task of relaxing your body. Freed from this task, the mind may now be subject to the normal barrage of unwanted or negative thoughts. There is a simple, natural principle that can be applied to overcome this problem so that you can achieve the required peace of mind:

You cannot think of
two things at the same time.

Making use of this law is very easy. All you need to do is direct your attention away from the distractions by giving it something else on which to concentrate. Soft music is one possibility, or an interesting narrative on tape. The easiest way is to cast your mind back in time to some pleasant event, such as a holiday, and to relive this in the imagination. This may be done with your eyes open or closed. It does not matter how you choose to do this, because the main consideration is to be comfortable, rather than seeking to conform to some rigid technique.

Another possibility is to imagine a purely fictitious scene, suggestive of peace and tranquillity. An imaginary beach or a woodland scene are two possibilities, but of course you must choose your own. Spend some time letting your mind wander within this imaginary scene until you feel peaceful and calm. The exact amount of time varies from person to person. There are no hard and fast rules.

Learning to relax fully may, at first, be a slow process. Eventually, you will be able to relax fully in a few moments, if you persist. The next stage is to use the imagination in a much more powerful way. The pictures you have been constructing in your mind have, without your knowledge, been affecting your inner mind, for the simple reason that these pictures also carry an instruction—that of seeking peace of mind. Look at the difference between daydreaming and the deliberate use of imaginary pictures to achieve an effect, in this case tranquillity. With daydreaming, there is no purpose other than to escape. With this exercise, there is an *intention*. The pictures are related to that intention, albeit in an indirect way. Now we will use the imagination in conjunction with a specific intention—that of increasing your money supply.

The relaxation exercise should have gone a long way toward removing worries and other distractions. It is most important that these negative thoughts not intrude. Again, practice makes perfect. So don't give up if, at first, you experience some difficulties. Eventually, you will learn to master these problems with ease. If you achieve nothing else, you will have learned how to remain calm and how to rid yourself of needless worry and anxiety. Negative thoughts such as these are not only upsetting, they are also counterproductive, because the mental pictures you erect while doing this have an effect on your inner mind. They are, in fact, acting as instructions. Little wonder that worry solves nothing. In fact, it does exactly the reverse. Realize that worry causes you to think in pictures and also realize that there is a powerful intention behind these thoughts, an intention that is bound to get results, even if they are not what you really want. Look carefully at negative thoughts. While indulging in them, you are really admitting to yourself that the situation is hopeless, that there is nothing to be done, that here is no hope, that a solution is impossible. You are practicing the art of belief without knowing it and, as you now know, whatever you believe to be true *becomes* true.

As you examine the relaxing technique used here, note how natural it is. First think about something until you become so involved that pictures appear in your mind and you start to be emotionally involved with them. The more you think, the greater the emotional effect, until the idea becomes all-absorbing. It is quite effortless! All you need do is think of bills, debts, or threatening letters and, before long, you are completely absorbed in the subject. At the back of this is a firm belief that disaster is just around the corner. Naturally, nothing seems to go right because you are not expecting matters to improve. You have spent so much time indulging in your own version of what the future holds that you would be amazed if anything happened to the contrary! Now can you see what persistent practice can do? With negative thinking, you devote most of your everyday life to indulging in a vision of the future that is false, but that you are making very real. Think what would happen if you simply changed the vision from a negative one to a positive one. And be sure that you put as much effort into it. You could not fail. The truth is that you never fail to get what you see in your mind and what you think about constantly. The *quality* of your thinking, however, determines what kind of results you get in physical terms. It is important, therefore, to look at the way you think about what life appears to offer and, of course, what you want from it.

Getting an instruction through to the inner mind is an easy affair. You have been doing it all your life, albeit in the wrong way. Now is the time to take control. Look at what happens. First comes thinking, then imaginary pictures, followed by emotional reactions. In negative terms, this would equate to brooding over some problem. In positive terms, this is known as creative visualization.

You can practice creative visualization anytime, anywhere. There are no special times to worry or get depressed. By the same token, creative visualization is not bound by any special times or places. As long as you are awake, you can use your mind.

Remember that it is important to be positive at all times. Keep reminding yourself of this and you will soon get into the habit. Above all else, disregard the apparent and the obvious for the simple reason that, if you continue to think about these as "reality," they will remain real. The important thing to bear in mind is that you must now start to think about what you *want* and you must think about it as though it were not only possible, but actual fact. Do not try to tell me that you cannot. I know that you can if you try. Your mind is a tool. To make use of it, you will need to practice and overcome bad habits. You will not do this overnight, but you can always succeed if you persist. So resolve to do so at all costs.

Chapter 12

Needs and Desires

What is it that you want? Obviously this will vary from person to person, so it is difficult for me to be precise here. You must therefore decide for yourself. However, here are a few guidelines. Money is simply a unit of exchange. It buys goods and services. If you had enough money, what would you buy? A new car, a bigger house, a long holiday? Think about these things. While doing this, do not restrict yourself by applying or accepting limitations. Remember that the only limits the inner mind understands are those that you give it. A good idea is to pretend that you have an unlimited amount of money so you can buy whatever you like. Think expansively. The more you do, the better the result.

Let your mind run freely over these ideas and you will then know what you want. Prior to this exercise you had no idea of what you wanted. If you are uncertain, how can your inner mind give you anything better? You will soon begin to realize that your ideas about money were extremely limited. All you ever seriously thought about was earning a living, paying the bills, and perhaps putting a little to one side for the future. You will soon see that this vision of the future is both unreal and self-restricting. This is an image that you believe to be true—therefore it *is* true for you. Be expansive, think "big," and let the old images give way to new ones. An additional advantage to thinking like this is that you are, in a way, giving instructions to your inner mind, because you are starting to define new horizons and expand the old limits. Think deeply about these matters, make written lists and notes, and get involved with the basic idea. The more you do, the better the result.

What Do You Want?

There are only three kinds of failures. One results from the ineffective pursuit of well-defined goals. One results from working aggressively toward ill-defined goals. The third, and the saddest of them all, results when neither well-defined goals nor effective pursuit is present.

Look at what is going on in your mind. So often people do not know what they want. Their will is not firm, there are too many confusions, too many contradictions. One of the golden rules of creative visualization is therefore: before doing any creative work, think of what you want and think it out carefully. This process is a very important one. Because the thinking that is going on in your imagination is all going into your memory, courtesy of the inner mind. So your memory has all that information stored in it, as well as your thinking about all your desires, and your fears, and so on. At the end of the day, however, it will have the one thing that matters—a decision. And that will be stored away for future use.

Setting Goals

In this exercise, you will create a list of all those things for which you have an immediate need. Imagine that someone has offered to provide for your every need. This is the list you would hand them. Figure 5 (see page 89) gives some examples, but you should be creative in developing your own list. Put everything you need on your list. Do not think in a "limited" manner. To make it easier, you can, if you like, write down five or six of your most important needs. Remember you can change and revise this list at any time.

Things I Need

Suggestions:	I Need:
Rent or mortgage payment	_____
New furniture	_____
Bills paid	_____
New stove	_____
Medical insurance	_____
Regular income	_____
New job	_____
New clothes	_____
Medical operation	_____
Car repair	_____
New washing machine	_____
Dental work	_____
Own apartment or house	_____
or anything necessary to	_____
satisfy your current	_____
requirements	_____

Figure 5. Sample list of things you need.

When you have completed this list, you can move on to the next—a list of things you desire. This is not a list of things you need, but a list of things you desire—and the sky's the limit. Include everything you want now or might want sometime in the future. (See figure 6, page 91, for a sample list.) You can have long- or short-term goals—one-year, three-year, five-year, and so on—that can ultimately lead to your accomplishing everything on your list. Whether your goals are short- or long-term, be sure they are in sync with your overall blueprint for a successful life. In other words, be sure that they can be made to materialize in a gradual step-by-step process. Do not take on too much at once.

It is clear that you desire more than material possessions. These do not constitute the sum-total of a successful life. You need certain qualities and attributes of personality. You need intangible characteristics to guarantee your success. You therefore need to make one more list, one of personal qualities you need (see figure 7, page 92).

Once you have created these lists, when you start to deliberately activate your inner mind, it will already have a clear-cut decision to act upon, plus the support of all your previous thinking. If you just do a creative visualization in an unthinking way, without the forethought required to make these lists, you may cause problems. Your inner mind really does not know what you want. It is not directed by a decision. It doesn't have a clear-cut purpose. Looking at this broadly, the first thing to do is to look at your entire life—at all the things you really want and need and, of course, those things you no longer want. Imagine that you really do have unlimited power, unlimited funds. Let your imagination be s-t-r-e-t-c-h-e-d to the limit and start to write down a list of all these desires. You can divide them into two categories, if you like—into needs and desires. If your health is not very good, you obviously need better health more than you need or desire a better car. Put these needs and desires into order of priority; think about these things constantly.

Things I Desire

Suggestions:	I Desire:
New car "Mercedes"	_____
$500,000 in the bank	_____
My own business	_____
A successful marriage	_____
A world cruise	_____
A country house	_____
A luxury yacht	_____
A vacation hideaway	_____
Own property abroad	_____
To get out of debt	_____
Spend more quality time with my family	_____
Better health	_____
_____	_____
_____	_____

Figure 6. Sample list of things you desire.

Personal Qualities I Need and Desire

Suggestions:	I Need and Desire:
More self-confidence	_____
To stop "putting things off"	_____
Ability to finish what I start	_____
To be in good health	_____
More original thinking-creativity	_____
To stop "wasting time"	_____
To have more courage	_____
To attract more friends	_____
To be more aggressive	_____
To have more perseverance	_____
To achieve more goals	_____
To have an excellent memory	_____
To be enthusiastic	_____
To be an excellent speaker	_____
To be the center of attention	_____
To be at ease in the company of the opposite sex	_____
To be a leader	_____

Figure 7. Sample list of personal qualities you need and desire.

It is important that you write all your goals out in a correct way. This is a prime requirement for your success.

1. Be sure that your needs or desires don't contradict each other. (In other words, do you want a champagne lifestyle with a beer salary?) Solution: raise your income goal.

2. Express your needs and desires in complete detail. (Do not just write "a new car." Get involved with the desire, listing every detail, as though you had to depend on this description alone, after giving the company your cash!)

3. Make sure your needs and desires are realistic. (Is it possible for a human being to achieve or do it?)

4. State each goal as if it were already accomplished. (In other words, are the goals you worded expressed in the imperative: "I have . . . I am . . . I own.")

Spend as much time as you like on this, but write it down. This is the way the mind works. We have lost the ability to believe and now we have to regain it.

Your inner mind responds to your wishes, to your directions but it only does this in specific ways. For instance, it does not understand the spoken language unless it is emotionally charged and used with symbolism. It responds to pictures that are put in the mind. Mind power *is*. It works because you sustain a picture in your mind of the very thing that you want and you ignore the apparent facts. By doing this positively, by believing in that imagery, by indulging in it, you make it happen. If you want to acquire a new car, sit down and think about the car that you want: the color, the make, the upholstery, the mileage it gets. Look at this in your mind's eye, in your imagination. You do not have to have your eyes closed, or actually see this car. You can do this work imaginatively, by thinking about the car. Gradually that mental picture becomes more and more firm in your mind. Then take it one stage further. Give your inner mind the positive instruction that reflects what you want. You do this by actually affirming the image in your mind, by imagining that you actually have a car, that you are driving it, that you are looking at it, you feel the upholstery.

Indulge in this vision. Do this every day. Persist with this particular image and within a very short period of time, through perfectly natural channels, it starts to materialize. In fact, it will turn up in the most surprising ways. The mistake is to look at the obvious—"I could never afford the deposit," "I cannot afford to run it." That is the normal human way of looking at things, but that, as you will see, is the wrong way. The correct way is to adopt an approach of believing in an image. If you do this within a correctly symbolic pattern, one that the inner mind understands—what we call the cosmic sphere—the process is accelerated considerably, because you are providing your inner mind with a master key that opens the doors to power.

As you go on through this book, take each of your own problems, each of your desires, and pinpoint them exactly. Apply your inner-mind power to each one of these things, and the results will be inevitable. Inevitability should be a keyword in creative visualization. My idea is that everybody finds out who they are and what they are capable of creating by using their creative abilities.

Chapter 13

Images and Power

In the next stage, you will add more power to your images. This is not difficult, if practiced with persistence and in a relaxed state of mind. You now know what you want. All that remains is to learn how to instruct the inner mind to get it for you. Keep the truth in mind. Go over it in your mind, if necessary, so that it is absolutely clear. One way to do this is to put your image into a statement that may then be written down and read. Alternatively, memorize this statement and then repeat it, either aloud or silently, in your mind. Here is a suggestion you may choose to adopt, or you may invent alternative methods of your own.

The following words are statements of fact and should be treated as such. Do not simply repeat these words without thought, perhaps hoping that they *may* be true. This is the wrong way to approach matters. Words are very important, because they can so easily affect the inner mind—if used properly. Some of you may have read or heard about "words of power." Words of power are words that have been *given* power. If English is your native language, use it. Words spoken in ancient Hebrew, Greek, or Latin will mean nothing to your inner mind, simply because you do not understand them. And if you do not understand them, how on Earth can you use them to communicate instructions to your inner mind? Forget about so-called words of power, strange "ancient" chants, or whatever else may be peddled as "powerful" incantations, proven "spells," or "guaranteed" invocations. I assure you that they work rarely, if at all! Real words of power are simply words containing a hidden something extra—sincerity.

The Creed of Truth

In the first instance, there is life-energy, constantly outpouring, without beginning or end. It is abundant and designed to be used creatively.

In the second instance, there is my inner mind, which acts as a mediator for the life-energy. It is my friend and my servitor. It seeks only to assist and to answer questions truthfully. It knows no limits, other than those I choose to define. It can and does affect circumstances, events, and physical matter in accordance with the instructions I give it. It will therefore never fail me.

In the third instance, there is my will to determine what the future should or should not be and the absolute truth of free choice. I am therefore bound by no beliefs other than those I choose to adopt.

In the fourth instance, there is physical matter, which is enlivened and given form by life-energies. By free choice and with the aid of my inner mind, matter must respond to my will.

Let me illustrate the point. You can buy an expensive book on magick that gives just the right spell you are looking for. You can then chant this spell until the cows come home, or the Sun goes cold, and nothing will happen. You can speak it in quiet tones or shout it loud enough to burst blood vessels and still nothing will happen. Why? Apart from the fact that you have been misled, you did not put in the "hidden extra," that unknown factor that makes the difference between success and failure. From this point of view alone, all these chants, word-spells, and invocations are ineffective. I would not waste my breath on them. Neither will you, once you realize the truth.

Let me give you an example of how words of power work. Take the statement, "I am rich." It is just a series of spoken words and, as such, it is ineffective. Now say these same words slowly and deliberately, with feeling, believing them to be true, while, at the same time, using your imagination to see yourself actually being rich. Repeat the words over and over until you feel rich and are confident that the words are true. Do you see the difference? These now become "words of power" by virtue of the fact that sincerity and belief have given them impetus. Believe in the truth of what you say, and it shall become fact.

You can also use "The Creed of Truth" (page 96). Memorize it. Say it to yourself often, until it becomes part of your everyday thinking. When reading or saying it, do so with conviction, with belief. Use your imagination and put feeling into these words.

Adding Power to Your Mental Images

To add more power to your mental images, relax as described and use The Creed of Truth to bring truth into your mind. The next stage is to think with intention. Obviously, different people have different intentions. You should adopt your intentions based on your own particular needs.

The first thing to do with any creative working is to get the intention firmly fixed in your mind. So often, people wander into creative visualization work without really knowing what they want. Their will is not set; there are too many confusions. So the golden rule is: Before any creative visualization work, think of what you want and think it out carefully. This process is a very important one, because any thinking that is going on in your imagination is going into your memory, courtesy of the inner mind. Your memory, consequently, is storing all your desires and your fears. At the end of the day, however, it will also have the one thing that matters—a decision—stored away for future use.

You can either do a blanket ritual that covers most of your desires, or you can do a complete ritual that runs over all of the things you are trying to bring about. Or you can narrow your working down to one possibility. Whatever you do, think it out very carefully, so there are no doubts or uncertainties, no negative thoughts that are likely to crowd in. All these things should be taken care of beforehand.

Before you start, it is important that you relax and become unaware of the outside world and any possible distractions. These can be your first stumbling block. Sitting in your bedroom, always conscious that someone might walk in, will not do. You have to find some way of making your position secure, so that you do not have to worry about disturbances. By doing this, you will be able to relax more, and the more you relax, the more efficient your creative work.

Before you start any creative working, do all the preparatory thinking. There is nothing worse than being halfway through your creative visualization, just reaching a crucial point, and realizing that you haven't thought it through. Say you are visualizing for healing and your mind starts to bother you with questions like, "Am I entitled to this healing," "Would this be good for me?" or "Can this person really be healed?" All that sort of thinking should be done first. Thinking actually is the last thing that you should take in to a creative operation. You should rather take in a calm confidence and a purpose—

not thinking. Use your imagination. You do not have to visualize; you just pretend and make believe. Allow it to work—"allow" being the operative word. You have to adopt an attitude of calm confidence, almost indifference (although indifference is the wrong word). You must convince yourself that you "could not care less." Trust your inner mind; trust your inner self. Once you have done the thinking, your inner self knows exactly what you want. You do not have to reason with it any more. Trust it and let it work. Just allow it to work using a calm, confident attitude and you will be amazed at the results.

Getting Results

It is very important to start "small." Quite often, people leap in and want to win a lottery jackpot, or land themselves a million dollars, or marry somebody like Demi Moore. The net result is that there is a "credibility" gap. In this case, you are not dealing with a belief, but with a hope, a wish, or even an ideal that may start to stretch your imagination a bit too far. It is best to start small and build slowly and certainly on each success. In that way, you stand a far better chance of succeeding.

In dealing with the inner mind, always remember that, like a bird flying high in the sky, it can see all the obstacles, problems, and possibilities. It can also see the easiest way around them. This is particularly important. Always credit your inner mind with total power and insight. You may not be able to see a solution or a way out due to negative conditioning or a restricted perspective. But your inner mind has a global perspective. It can see all, even if you cannot. Once it accepts an instruction, it will find the quickest and best way to manifest this. Another factor to bear in mind is flexibility. It is a mistake to narrow down the possibilities. By doing so, you apply restrictions. Let me give you an example.

With continued practice, the inner mind will achieve results that may surprise you. Keep two points in mind. First, after the initial enthusiasm has worn off, you may be tempted to let things slide. Resist this at all costs. It is vitally important that you not only find time to practice these exercises, but persist in them. Resist temptation to give up if nothing appears to happen immediately, or to dash out and try something else. Persist, stay on course, and practice each day without fail. You will find, as have others, that there are numerous distractions that may tempt you to put off the effort, and an equal number of excuses that your mind may try to offer to abandon it. Ignore them, and resolve to continue past the point where others might give up. If you make a promise to yourself to persist and stick to this, you will win. There is no such thing as "instant" success. Everything takes time, and the time required to realize some definite result can not easily be calculated. To give up is folly. Persist at all costs. Eventually, you are bound to succeed.

You must also be ever-watchful of your general attitude. There is little point to spending half an hour each day in positive creative visualization and then spending the rest of the day (and perhaps a restless night) allowing yourself to become depressed, letting misery and other negative thoughts take over. The purpose of these exercises is primarily to change your dominant inner thoughts so that you can eventually form better habits of continuous positive thinking.

So, what is to be done? Resolve to resist these thoughts. At first, it will be difficult, because the habits of a lifetime are not so easily broken. Get into new habits. Every time negative thoughts creep in, push them to one side. Remember the truth about life, life-energies, the inner mind, and your ability to alter circumstances to deliver what you really want. Remember also that you cannot think of two things at the same time. So if you concentrate on knowing that you will succeed, knowing that you can win, knowing that what you see in your mind must happen, if you fill your mind with positive ideas and stubbornly refuse to entertain ideas to the contrary, if you believe in who you are and what you can achieve, and refuse point-blank to indulge in the supposed "facts" or the "obvious," you cannot fail. Living creatively is not a part-time affair or a hobby. It is a way of life. It is the same with these exercises. Because they are a way to shape reality, they must be treated with respect and must be integrated into your lifestyle. Such is the way of bending reality to our liking. There are no shortcuts, no "instant" solutions, no rapid formulas for success. All must be worked for. Always bear in mind that creative visualization is not something that you can take lightly. It is a way of life. The more you put in, the more you will get out of it.

As a practical suggestion, I advise you to perform creative visualization each day. By far the best time is in the morning, before the pressures of the day begin. It is also a good idea to practice your visualization at night, just before you drop off to sleep. It does not matter if you drift off to sleep while doing this. In fact, it will probably help matters by carrying these powerful thoughts over into your sleep state. Here, they will pass into the inner mind quite easily. If you have had restless nights worrying over money or other problems, you know the power of thoughts carried over into sleep. Negative thoughts disturb your sleep because they are still working on inner levels. Positive thoughts can have the opposite effect, if given a chance to do so.

If you ever assumed that the imagination was of no importance, as do most people, you should now begin to realize that this is not the case. Your imagination is a powerful tool, not to be dismissed so lightly. Remember that your mind is a tool, that thought affects matter and therefore circumstances. The correct way to change circumstances is to use the positive power of your mind, not worrying or trying to correct matters in other ways. The use of your imagination is all-important in this task.

To sum up: creative visualization is the science of using and understanding the vast potential of the inner mind. It responds to certain kinds of thinking. Learning how to use these kinds of thinking is therefore what creative visualization is really all about.

The inner mind is limitless in its ability to handle power, otherwise known as life-energy. It has total insight, is in direct contact with true wisdom, and, above all else, seeks only to serve. But this service is dependent on beliefs. What you believe to be true, is true. Your inner mind does not make moral distinctions, labeling things as "good" or "bad." You decide what is good or bad. Your inner mind simply acts on these judgments.

Your inner mind accepts instructions that are believed to be true. It is, therefore, vitally important that you be careful in what you choose to believe. You have free choice to believe or not to believe, whichever you like, because free choice is your right. Use it wisely and you will gain. The alternative is to accept wrong beliefs and thereby perpetuate needs and negative attitudes.

Most people suffer from the delusion that it is difficult to believe, yet they have had, and still have, little problem believing all manner of incorrect assumptions, resumptions, and so-called facts—not to mention the fallacies put forward by hard-line rationalists. Let me define what belief actually is and how to acquire the skill to direct it.

First, focus on a thought. Hold on to it, regardless of any apparent "evidence" to the contrary that may be embodied in present circumstances, what others may think, or what you may previously have believed to be true. Keep this thought in your mind; hold to it; have faith in it; defy anything that stands in its way. It will not be long before this thought is accepted by your inner mind. Once this happens, it is bound to come true. While doing this, your conscious, rational mind will give all manner of excuses as to why this line of thought should be abandoned. But these are only conscious thoughts, and should be disregarded. This takes patience and practice, but it does work, if you are persistent and unflinching in your aims. There are no "temptations of the flesh," so to speak. The only real temptations are those that exist in your mind—the temptations to give up and return to the "norm," whatever that may be. Resist these until you win. Then you will know, firsthand, of the real truth and the power of the mind.

You often read or hear about "willpower." Most think that this is beyond them, is for the talented few, or is, at best, very difficult to exert. To assert your willpower is simply to make up your mind that you want something, and then refuse to be put off. In short, think about what you want and hold to that thought. Believe in it as a reality, regardless of what may appear to be true. This is willpower in action, and anyone can do it.

The art of creative visualization first takes control of the conscious (doubting) mind by calming it down and refusing to let it be the victim of worry and other negative thoughts. Calmness is a major key in creative visualization, hence the ideas given to you concerning relaxation. If you are calm, there is less chance that distracting thoughts may flood your mind and make matters worse. Only with a calm mind can you begin to see clearly and/or give instructions to your inner mind. Panic, anxiety, or depression are bad habits. They are nonproductive, in real terms. Get into a new habit of slowing down and thinking positively and creatively, as suggested. At first, you may well have to do this many times a day, because old habits die hard. But with constant practice—in other words, by exercising your will—the new habit will take over. Not only will this help you to gain better results in physical terms, it will also have a noticeable effect on your general health. Controlling your mind has many benefits, if you choose to reap them.

Practice this, together with creative visualization, each and every day. Think about what you want rather than letting your mind dwell on what you do not want. Let your imagination work positively, as suggested. Believe in these new thoughts and you cannot fail. These are the first principles of creative visualization.

Chapter 14

The Four Gateways of Reality

People instinctively look toward the sky for inspiration and for answers to their problems. In a way, they are right to look upward, for our problems exist in higher planes, in the misdirected energy patterns within our inner minds. These energy patterns are not external. They are part of us all. Therefore, any problems are naturally caused by the higher parts of ourselves, parts that are out of tune with the reality of our true selves. The lesson of physicality is therefore quite simple: Outer conditions are the results of inner thinking. Thus, the solution to our problem, is in the problem itself. Not only is the cosmic sphere equivalent to the physical world, it is the idealistic state in which we must work to reshape our reality. The symbols for physicality are the "encircled cross" and the "four elemental gateways" of (virtual) reality. Through these gateways or doorways, we contact and use the power of the elements, allowing that power to produce physical results.

As I have already said, the cosmic sphere is a three-dimensional inner state. This is the true cosmic circle in which your secret temple of the mind is situated (more on this later). You have already been shown the correct way to construct this sphere in your own imagination. You need little practice, however, in order to become proficient. This can be done at anytime and requires no special paraphernalia or equipment. Start by becoming calm and reasonably relaxed, then construct the cosmic sphere in your mind. Imagine that you are standing in the center of a huge sphere traced out in shining light. Do not strain to see this. Simply imagine that it is there. As a useful aid to concentration, try keying this in with a short phrase that acts as a command, such as:

Circle of Cosmos, Arise.

Now erect the triple rings of the cosmos and see yourself standing within their center. Remember that magical or imaginary east, as it is known, is always in front of you when "opening" the cosmic sphere. This need not be in alignment with true east indicated by a compass. To return to normal (and this is just as important), just reverse the process by using another phrase to dismiss the sphere:

Circle of Cosmos, Depart.

As you say this, watch the cosmic sphere disappear in the customary fashion. With a little practice, you will become familiar with this procedure and then you can move on to the next stage. This involves the idea of the four gateways of reality and should be practiced carefully.

Working with the Vital Four Gateways of Reality

Once again, become calm, then open the cosmic sphere as directed. Now imagine that at each of the four points of the compass there is a doorway that can be opened or closed at will. Through these symbolic doorways flows life-energy that can be directed to obtain the results you desire. Treat this exercise seriously. Spend some time using your imagination to see these opening and closing at your command. It is often a good idea to use simple phrases as keywords. As a suggestion try, "Let the portals be opened." To close, use, "Let the portals be closed." Naturally, you may use whatever wording you desire;

there is no need to use my words. At conclusion of this exercise, close the cosmic sphere as usual.

The exercise just given should not be rushed, nor should it be treated as pointless. Remember that you are dealing with your mind and that your mind is a tool. With practice, your inner mind will obey your visualizations and realize that you are taking control if this power. Like any skill involving the use of tools, patience and practice is needed to obtain the best results.

Attracting an Abundance of Natural Energy into Your Life

The final stage should also be practiced carefully. It uses The Creed of Truth in conjunction with this subjective symbol pattern (see page 96). Relax, clear the mind, and then open the cosmic sphere. Repeat the creed, either out loud or silently in your mind, bringing in the added dimension of the symbolic doorways with the following words:

In the first instance, there is life-energy, constantly outpouring, without beginning or end. It is abundant and is designed to be used creatively.

[Imagine that the eastern doorway now opens. Use a command phrase, if desired. Remember that the eastern doorway is in front of you.]

In the second instance, there is my inner mind that acts as a mediator for life-energy. It is my servitor and seeks only to assist and to answer questions truthfully. It knows no limits, other than those I choose to define. It can and does affect circumstances, events, and physical matter, in accordance with the instructions I give it. It will therefore never fail me.

[Imagine that the southern doorway now opens.]

In the third instance, there is my will to determine what the future should or should not be and the absolute truth of free choice. Therefore, I am bound by no beliefs other than those I choose to adopt.

[Imagine that the western doorway now opens.]

In the fourth instance, there is physical matter, which is enlivened and given form by life-energies. By free choice and with the aid of my inner mind, matter must respond to my will.

[Imagine that the northern doorway now opens.]

Remember, if words are used, they work only because you put feeling, belief, and imagination into them. For instance, if you are facing a particular quarter and simply say, "I declare this quarter open," you will not succeed. It is one thing to say the words and not think about them. It is another entirely to see vividly in your imagination the doorway that exists on that particular quarter opening and colored energy pouring through it. Say the words with feeling and imagination, and you will work absolute wonders. The words, whatever they are, then become a vehicle for expressing emotion and imagination. There is a world of difference.

With practice, this exercise can provide a perfect framework for creative visualization, no matter what you may choose to work for. Try it now. The amount of time you spend on this is entirely up to you. There are no hard-and-fast rules, so let your own feelings and inclinations be your guide. The only rule that applies is that you cannot rush through these exercises. Success is governed by a simple formula: *input = output*. In short, what you get out of them varies in direct proportion to that which you put in. This has nothing to do with money. But it has everything to do with personal involvement and a small sacrifice of time and effort needed to gain results.

To close the exercise, use a command statement to close the doors. See this happen in your imagination, then close the cosmic sphere as described. This exercise is extremely effective by itself, but may be augmented by using additional aids, such as soft music, incense, joss sticks, or a "self candle," which is explained in chapter 16. These are not essential. They are mentioned only in passing. It is really all a question of balance. On the one hand, there is no point in looking for a cheap, "instant," get-rich-quick method, using only those parts of this book that appeal to you. On the other hand, there is also little point in spending a small fortune on supposed magical artifacts in the hope that these will, all by themselves, cause the heavens to pour forth abundance. In the final analysis, you must use your own judgment, relying on reason, knowledge, and common sense.

your work. The obvious remedy is not to tell anyone, unless they are also actively committed to realistic magical advancement and are therefore sympathetic. This, incidentally, is the real reason for magical secrecy.

What else can be done to improve matters? Electric lighting does little to promote calmness. Candlelight is far better. No need for special candles. An ordinary candle will work quite well. Apart from giving off natural light, this may also be used as a focus for attention. Spend some time looking at the flame and thinking about it, rather than letting your mind wander about, out of control. Use these items fully. Incense is always a valuable aid in calming the mind and you are urged to try it. There are two alternatives: loose incense, or stick incense, otherwise known as joss sticks. The former must be burned on specially produced charcoal blocks in some safe container. Specially made incense burners are available, but it is quite possible to use a metal or pottery dish containing a little sand or some other nonflammable substance on which the hot charcoal rests. Loose incense has the advantage of being available in a wide variety of scents. Moreover, you can judge exactly how much scent you wish to produce. Joss sticks, on the other hand, are very easy to use. All you need to do is light them with a match, blow out the flame, and let the perfume fill the room as the stick continues to smolder gently. Special holders can be purchased, or you can adapt everyday articles. Incense works by association. In other words, by working with a particular scent along a particular line, the scent comes to evoke a response in your mind. For example, if you are visualizing for wealth and wealth-related things, using sandalwood on a regular basis will eventually help bring to mind ideas of wealth. With candlelight and incense you can create a perfect setting for creative visualization.

Chapter 16

Your Inner Temple

When you have opened a creative visualization session using the cosmic rings (see page 69), you can make use of the four gateways and a little-known technique that involves the use of an "inner" temple, an imaginary temple that exists in your mind. This temple can be an extremely valuable and powerful aid.

People often look for things that are far too complicated. The inner temple concept may at first seem to be too simple and childlike. But that is characteristic of the inner mysteries. Creative visualization works best through simplicity. This book attempts to put everything in perspective and teach the true simplicity of "inner" workings. The inner temple exercise is a start.

The approach to inner working is often made in childlike terms. Remember Christ's words: "Verily I say unto you, whosoever shall not receive the kingdom of God as a little child, he shall not enter therein" (Mark 10:15). Although the inner temple concept may appear overly simple at first, you will see, as you proceed through this book, that its simplicity is its true virtue. Although ideas like this go against established custom, I think we have relied on established custom for far too long, and with far too few results. What we need is a new and original approach and a return to older and more valid ideas.

The inner temple is one such idea. It is an old technique, a very old technique. But it is relatively unknown in this day and age, and sadly neglected by most esoteric schools. The important thing, therefore, is not to treat it as something simple.

It is, I assure you, extremely powerful in its action, as you will see if you persist in its use.

The following exercise has the effect of increasing your contact with life-energies by supplying additional symbols to the existing scheme. Your inner mind will recognize these if they are practiced carefully and patiently. The end result is bound to be an ability to exert more effective control. In order to get maximum benefit from your creative visualization, however, I offer an additional piece of information that is quite original and probably unknown to most practitioners.

By establishing the cosmic sphere and the four gateways of the elements, we have constructed a power base that cannot fail to serve us well if used with purpose. The only thing lacking in our scheme is something to symbolize the center in our imagination. There are many obvious advantages in this, one being that, as the center is the inner mind, anything that symbolizes it is bound to be extremely powerful if used correctly.

The Magical Inner Temple

Having opened the four doorways, you need only imagine that you are standing inside an inner temple. The shape, size, and decor are entirely up to you. This is important, because any inner temple must be individual. It must be *your* inner temple. Spend some time thinking about this and give yourself lots of scope. Inner temples are many and varied. Some people like to imagine something similar to a church or cathedral, others prefer a castle or even a stone circle, or perhaps a pyramid. Take your time and allow ideas to arise in your mind.

The center of your inner temple is represented by a magical pool of water. This symbol is valid for a variety of reasons and will become a major factor in the success of your creative work. The use of the pool is fully discussed in the next chapter, when this simple idea will be put into effective practice.

A Ritual

To ritualize the cosmic sphere and inner temple is quite simple. The process is best divided into two stages. In the first, we move into the realms of ritual by erecting the cosmic sphere thus having an impact on the inner-mind levels. We use a candle to focus our attention.

Your Self Candle

Select a candle that will represent you. Do not rush out and buy any old candle. Think about this very carefully. What shape will it be? What size and what color? Take your time. Also, don't be influenced by what you have read elsewhere. It is your decision and you must come to this decision all by yourself.

Set up an altar (see page 111) and place the candle in its center. Sit down and spend some time relaxing and pushing aside any everyday thoughts—especially worries—until you are quite calm. When you are relaxed, stand up and light your self candle. Sit down and think about this candle. It represents you, not the ordinary you, but the *real you* (see page 25). Do you remember what the real you is? Cast your mind back over all that has so far been written concerning your inner mind and the power that you have at your command.

The next step is to think about all the things you have written on your needs and desires lists. Remember, do not restrict yourself in any way. Be completely positive and give your imagination free rein. Remember that, in truth, nothing is impossible. All you have to do is instruct your inner mind, and it is bound to come true.

It is very important not to let self-restricting ideas or beliefs get in the way of this process. Treat this as an enjoyable exercise at all times. Whenever you come up against any negative thoughts, such as, "I cannot," or, "If only," dismiss them and remember that you *can*. Never let the apparent "facts" get in the way. As you will see, these so-called facts can be changed.

Continue this exercise for as long as you like, performing it once a day. Not only will you learn a great deal about yourself and about life, you will also notice a difference in yourself. Keep up the practice and do not allow other matters such as, "I have not got the time today," to get in the way. If you want to change your life, you must be prepared to make some sacrifices and you must learn persistence and patience.

To close the exercise, extinguish the self candle and put everything away until the next session. It is a good idea to make lists of all the ideas that occur to you during a session. These lists can provide material for many rituals later on, for they reflect your intentions. Naturally, you can add to this list at any time. In fact, it is always a good idea to spend odd moments looking at them in order to decide what you really want. When you know what you really want, you are halfway down the path to actually getting it. So think about and practice these exercises regularly.

Stage One—The Cosmic Sphere

For this ritual, you will need your self candle (see page 119). This should be set up as before and you should relax completely before beginning.

Imagine your inner light becoming brighter and more powerful. Take your time and realize that this symbolizes your inner mind in action. Think about this while casting your mind over all that has been written here about the inner mind and its potential. Light the central candle, which now symbolizes this inner power. In other words, you now have a physical representation of this power, rather than a plain candle. From the flame, imagine that a beam of light rises upward to form the first path, terminating at the top of the sphere with the symbol of a crown. Similarly, imagine a beam of light traveling down toward the base, terminating with the symbol of a black cubic stone. This forms the second path. The central axis is now complete.

Again using the flame as the central point, see a beam of light go out toward imaginary east, terminating in a symbol of a sword. Do exactly the same with the other three arms of the cross, seeing a wand at the south, a cup at the west, and, finally, a shield at the north. To complete the procedure, use your imagination to see the three cosmic rings being formed. The cosmic sphere is now complete (see figure 8, below).

By completing the sphere, you have also divided life's energies into four distinct categories, each with its own symbolism to aid in identification. By focusing your mind on the sword, for instance, you can contact the element of air and all that this element represents. This is also true for the wand, the cup, and the shield. The sword is said to "rule" the element of air. This does not mean that, when you pick up a sword, the air element will automatically respond to your wishes. Only those who understand the air element and have worked with the inner symbol of the sword have the power to control and direct that element. The same rule applies to any of the other weapons.

The entire process depends on opening the temple. It will, with practice, serve to inform your inner mind that you wish to work creatively. If you view this as a sort of on/off

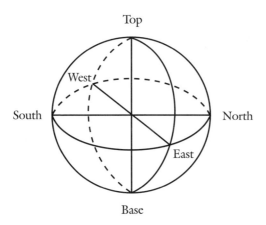

Figure 8. The triple rings of the cosmos.

switch, you will have a reasonable idea of its function. You should never omit temple openings (or closings) from any creative work if you truly wish to make good progress and, at the same time, avoid problems. Control is what you seek. And creation without control is both pointless or self-defeating. As in previous exercises, closing down is accomplished by reversing the procedure and returning to normal, everyday awareness. The opening effect puts your inner mind into a condition of readiness for whatever is to follow—the actual creative work itself. There is, however, an intermediary step that "activates" the cosmic sphere in a special way. This is not particularly difficult, although it requires some practice. It does not, however, require any additional equipment. It is done entirely through the imagination.

Practice this exercise often before you move on to the second stage. Do not rush through it. Take your time until you are familiar with the cosmic sphere and its construction. When you are satisfied with your proficiency, move on to Stage Two.

Stage Two—Your Inner Temple

In Stage Two, we move into the realm of virtual reality—the inner temple itself. First construct the cosmic sphere, thereby, in effect, putting your inner mind into a state of readiness. Having opened the creative session using the cosmic rings, you will now make use of a little-known technique that involves the inner temple. This is done in the imagination. All you need do is imagine that there is a strong door in front of you. On that door is your name, in the center of an encircled cross symbol. Reach out in your imagination and touch it. See the door open and walk through it. Feel yourself entering an enormous hall decorated in every color of the rainbow. In the center of this hall is a pool. Walk slowly toward it. You are now standing right in front of the central pool. Then light your self candle, which, of course, is a symbolic representation of your inner power (your inner mind). Contemplate this for a while.

In the next stage, you will bring in the idea of the four elements. It is not necessary that you understand the complexity of the fourfold system of power that exists within everything. What does matter is that you construct a symbolic representation of this system in your imagination. To do this, use your imagination once again to see another doorway in front of you. This door is yellow and represents the power of the air element. See the door open, letting a bright yellow light into your inner temple. Now imagine a red doorway to your right. This is the doorway of the fire element. See this door open, allowing red light to enter your inner temple. Now imagine a blue doorway immediately behind you. This is the door of the water element. See this door open, allowing blue light into your inner temple. Finally, to your left, see a green doorway that equates to the earth element. Open this door and allow green light to enter your inner temple.

Your inner temple has now been opened and is ready for creative visualization. I suggest that you burn some incense or joss sticks and once again consider your desires in the light of what has been written in this chapter. In other words, use creative visualization.

Spend as long as you like on this, remembering that input = output — put another way, practice makes perfect. The more you practice this basic procedure, the better. Through it, you stimulate you inner mind into action by using a symbol pattern that it understands. When you visualize, you are using the transmutation of the elements. Let me explain. Your imagination is the space within which the four elements are controlled and operate. The air element wants to move to a different location and, therefore, to relate to something else (thinking). The fire element wants to expand itself and therefore to consume (desire). The water element wants to flow downward and therefore to contract (image). The earth element is content to remain where it is and does not want to move or change to any other state (physical object). This can be summed up as: Think it (air), desire it (fire), see it (water), have it (earth).

To close the Inner Temple Exercise, use a closing formula. To do so, simply reverse the opening formula. Start by seeing the eastern (yellow) doorway of air close firmly. Do the same with south (red), west (blue), and north (green), in that order. All that remains to be done is to extinguish your self candle and see yourself going back through the original door through which you came. See this door close firmly. Return to normal consciousness. The closing is complete.

In summary, the procedure for creative visualization ought to be:

1. Open the creative working by erecting the cosmic rings, thereby establishing the cosmic sphere.

2. Use your imagination to see and enter the inner temple, and open the four gateways.

3. Focus your mind on the central pool and perform the main work—visualizing your intention.

4. To complete the work, close down by using your imagination to close the four gates and leave the inner temple. Then close down the sphere.

How to Visualize More Than One Thing at Once

You may wonder how it is possible to visualize the cosmic sphere, inner temple, gateways, and weapons all at once, not to mention staying focused on your intention. It is all a question of memory. To visualize several different things at the same time would, of course, be difficult, if not impossible. Fortunately, you do not need to do this. As you build up the cosmic sphere, you establish each part in your memory. As you move through each successive stage, you concentrate only on what is necessary to that stage. For example, start with the central light, visualizing that it exists. Then, move your attention on to the next stage of visualizing the rings and the cosmic sphere, entering the inner temple, opening the gateways, and so on. There is no need to keep the image of the cosmic sphere and inner temple in your imagination, because they are assumed to exist and, in fact, do exist in your memory. We use this and similar procedures in everyday life. For instance, suppose you are standing in a room facing a window. You see the window quite clearly. If you turned around to face the opposite wall, you would, of course, see the wall instead. However, you would still know that the window exists because you just saw it. In fact, you can recall it in your imagination because its image is stored in your memory. In a similar fashion, having become familiar with the room, you know what the room looks like in totality, without actually seeing this physically.

Exactly the same thing occurs with the cosmic sphere. Creating your inner temple and using inner seeing—in other words, using your power of visualization—builds up an imaginary room in your memory. All through the building-up process, you establish each stage in your memory before moving on to the next. Therefore, at the pool (or fountain, explained in the next chapter), you are free to concentrate on it, knowing that the inner temple, doorways, and weapons exist in your memory because you have put them there. At the end of the creative session, you simply inform your inner mind that they are no longer established, hence the need for a closing procedure. Never forget, however, that although the cosmic sphere and inner temple are imaginary, they should not be dismissed as worthless. This is not the case. Any deliberate erection of a symbolic pattern will have an effect on the inner mind, because you are using what is, in effect, a powerful language that the inner mind understands. It is, therefore, necessary to treat these symbols with respect, and practice and use them often.

Chapter 17

The Magical Pool and Fountain of Power

The four gateways that equate to the four elements allow power to enter to the inner temple symbolically as each quarter is addressed and each doorway opened using the appropriate part of The Creed and its magical weapon (see page 96). This power is then allowed in to the inner temple, finally focusing in the center.

The Magical Pool

At the center of the temple is the pool. Here we will take the pool to a different symbolic level. I advise practicing this technique a few times to master the idea of the four gateways. As you approach each quarter, imagine that there is a doorway there. Act this out in your mind using the appropriate symbology, such as the magical sword, wand, cup, or shield. See that gateway open and try to cultivate a feeling of allowing power to come in through that gateway. Imagine that this power is under your control. For example, when you are visualizing the eastern door, see that doorway open and the yellow light of air pour in. Feel it coming in as power. Do the same with the red light of the south, and continue the process until all four lights finally shine in the central pool. When you are finished, reverse the procedure.

This technique can also be used pragmatically in the initial stages. Moreover, there is a point in the creative working at which you can put your intention into the central pool concept. The pool is, in fact, a very important symbol. If it remains just a pool, however, you are dealing with stagnant water, so to speak. If you stick to that static symbol in your mind, albeit in a meditational capacity, your inner mind will understand. But if you change that pool into a fountain of light, a fountain of water, shimmering with light and power, you have created two symbols, one static, one dynamic. In other words, if you want to get any information from your visualization, if you are trying to discover or learn something, you can use the pool as a crystal ball. If you are intent on doing something in a pragmatic sense, you can use the idea of the fountain, so that its power becomes dynamic. It comes through the four gateways into the center of the pool. It erupts there as a fountain of pure power. That power goes out through the four gateways into the outside world, carrying your intention with it. Thus the symbol of the pool offers two possibilities: a positive one, represented by the fountain, and a receptive and meditational one, represented by the pool.

Dream Seeds

This is a useful piece of ritualistic practice. Light a candle recognizing that its lighting is symbolic. You are actually making the light symbolic of your inner self, your inner power. The candle flame represents your true power. It is a ritualistic action, done with magical intent. Now start your inner temple journey. When you get to the pool, use your imagination. "Pretend" is perhaps the best word. Imagine that you have taken your two lists with you. Take your list of needs and drop it into the pool. See the waters react, bubbling and swirling, sucking the list down into the depths of the pool. If you have a list of problems, let the eddying waters wash those problems away. Do not think about it. Just enjoy the experience. Let it happen in a matter-of-fact way. Now take the other list, the one containing your desires, and drop it into the pool. See the waters acting on your desires in a positive way. See the water bubble and effervesce. See it fill with golden light. Give your imagination full range. Enjoy the experience, and ignore your conscious mind. Treat the whole thing as a game, if you like, but a game with a great deal of purpose.

You are communicating with your inner mind, at this point. You are giving it an instruction. You are saying "do something about these problems, because, although I cannot, not from a physical level, you can." Your inner mind will get the point and, in a strange and natural way, these "seeds" you are sowing will bear fruit. Eventually, not overnight, but gradually, in a perfectly natural way, these things will start to work themselves out, through your inner-mind power.

When you have finished, extinguish the candle and come back to normal. Then put all this at the back of your mind, try not to think about it. If you do think about it, you will find that you are thinking negatively, that you are giving yourself reasons why this cannot happen. Just push these ideas away, or give yourself a very good argument as to why these thoughts are indeed negative and stupid. It is far better to put these things to the back of your mind and forget them. Your inner mind cannot be stopped by conscious negative thoughts. It can, however, be slowed down. But if you leave it to get on with the job—in other words, if you have faith in it—that belief will empower it. Now you see the power of belief. If you do something with intent, if you act as if it is already done, you do not have to bother about it anymore. Then, strangely enough, the result will start to work out in your everyday life. This is what creative visualization is all about. As I have said, this simple approach is rather unorthodox. I believe, however, that far too much emphasis is being placed today on ritualistic procedure. As a result, people have forgotten about the magic of belief, the true magic of inner working.

The Magical Fountain

The magical fountain is a further extension of the pool symbol. Having opened the inner temple, keep your intention in mind. Now, imagine each of the elemental doorways opening. As they do, light or power, in the appropriate color, enters the inner temple and lights up the central pool. Impress your intention into the pool using a simple keyword, such as "love," "money," or "health." See this word on the surface of the pool or imagine that you are writing it in the water with your finger. Your inner mind will always know the purpose of the intention or desire. Use your own ideas and preferences to help personalize the creative operation.

Now see the pool turn into a fountain of water, glowing with the same colors. Visualize your desire amid all this energy, then see the inner temple fill with the same light, which then passes out through the four elemental doorways into the outside world. Pause for a while to contemplate this, remembering to be positive and to use creative visualization. To close the exercise, see the fountain revert back to a calm pool once more. See the light disappear, then close the temple and cosmic rings as previously described.

A lot of people make the mistake of expecting an instant reaction to their visualization. There is no such thing as an "instant" reaction. Everything takes time. The time required depends largely on the cosmic tides, the amount of creative visualization that you put into your work, and, of course, the severity of your inner problems. It is far better to allow time for something to happen. In the latter stages, as you get more proficient, you can put far more into your work and be more demanding: for example, "This is going to happen within a week!" In the initial stages, give things time to materialize. Remember, as well, that one creative visualization session does not necessarily do the trick. In the initial stages, because of lack of experience or negative thinking, your first try may not be successful. It is far better to use a back-up procedure. That can consist of simply keeping your idea or intention in mind, but keeping it in mind positively.

In other words, if you are visualizing to pass an exam, it may pay to spend some time each day sitting down quietly and, using the triple rings, run over your intention to succeed in your mind. Visualize that you are going to pass this particular exam. See this in your imagination as though it were true. Be totally positive. If you experience negative feedback from your conscious mind, stimulated from inner levels, this repetition gives you an opportunity each day to push it to one side. This leaves the channel open. If the cosmic rings and inner temple are performed correctly, they stimulate positive energy. But negative thinking can get in the way and slow things down. Sometimes it can slow things so drastically that you miss an opportunity. It pays to practice creative visualization using a sound power base. Concentrate at least each day on what you want, until you eventually succeed.

Chapter 18

Setting a Time Limit for Achieving Success

Setting a time limit for success is a matter of personal preference. I personally do set a time limit and I always achieve my objective before the time limit expires. Setting a time limit is a matter of expressing confidence. Do you believe in yourself and what you are doing enough to make it happen? Do you have the courage to say: "I am going to achieve it by a certain date," and know that it will be so? People have said to me: "You must have had failures in the beginning." No! I have never failed. I have always achieved or acquired what I wanted. I am naturally asked how, by which system, through which gods or masters. My system is my own. I use no gods, except the concept of a creative source. In my religion, there are only three people: "Me, myself, and I." I know "me." I have faith in myself, and in the power that is I. Does that sound arrogant? It is not meant to be. For that knowledge, once recognized, is not arrogance, nor is it humility. It is not pride, nor is it servitude. It just is. It is an awareness, a recognition of self, placed within the patterns of time and space.

The ideas in Part four are best left until you are an adept—in other words, until you have complete confidence in yourself. Remember that you are unlikely to succeed by performing just one creative operation. It is far better to perform the same creative visualization over a fixed period—a week, ten days, a fortnight. Persistence is the thing that matters in the early stages. By persisting, you are more likely to get a response from subconscious levels than you will be by pinning all your hopes on a single shot.

It is especially important for beginners not to set time limits on their objectives. The reasons for this are very complex. Simply concentrate on your purpose for a set number of visualizations and then await results, allowing natural forces to do their job along natural channels, which may have a time line all of their own. As long as you keep the channels open by being positive and by expecting a result, something is bound to happen.

Part
Four

Creative Visualizations

Chapter 19

Money

In order to increase your money supply, it is first necessary to look at the reasons for its apparent deficiency. It is important to look at these reasons because they are the cause of your need. Resist the temptation to just skim through this chapter in order to get the "secret," or to ignore these ideas, assuming that they are not important. Have patience and think about the ideas presented to you. This is not just a question of learning how to acquire more money. It is also vital that you understand what the problems are, why they happen, and how you can prevent them from standing in the way of continued success. There is an old magical truth that states that it is not just a question of learning how to contact and use power, it is also a case of unlearning faulty concepts, ideas, and ideals. This is just as true in life as it is in using your creative abilities. So take heed. Learn all, or risk failure.

The Value of Money

There are many misconceptions about money, about its value and how much or how little of it we are entitled to have. We will look at these in some detail in an effort to expose them for what they really are—fallacies.

Have you ever thought about what money really is, what it does, or where it comes from? Your attitude toward money is most important. Money is simply a unit of exchange. It buys things. Unless it is used, it is simply useless pieces of metal and paper. Money is potential—the more of it you have, the more you can potentially purchase. Always think of money in terms of purchasing power, in terms of what you can do with it, otherwise you run the risk of falling into grave error. The truth about money is that, in and of itself, it is quite useless. You think not? Ask any refugee in a war-torn country. They may well have a pocketful of money, or even gold and jewels. Because of the prevailing situation, however, it is valueless. They cannot buy anything, because no one will accept currency. Money, by itself, is quite worthless.

We can learn a very important lesson from this. First, to seek money simply for the sake of having it is quite pointless. All you would do is acquire pieces of paper. What is the point, unless you can do something with it? It may look very good on a bank statement, or piled up in front of you, but unless you intend to use it, it is wasted. Its potential is lost. This brings me to the second point. Most people are "security-mad." In other words, their idea of wealth is one of hoarding up money in the bank, or in some strange place such as under the mattress, as a hedge against adversity. Remember the parable of money: "For I say unto you, that unto every one which hath shall be given; and from him that hath not, even that he hath shall be taken away from him" (Luke 19:26). Such behavior is not only silly, it is immature. Stagnant money loses its potential. Worse still—and you can see this happen every day—are the poor unfortunates who spend most of their lives hoarding money for a "rainy day," and die and lose out anyway. What is the point? There is no point.

If you must have money, at least be prepared to think of it in terms of what it can do, what it can buy, and how it can be used to enhance your life and the lives of others. By giving to "others," I do not mean that, through some sense of guilt, you should seek to relieve yourself of a portion of your wealth in order to have a clean conscience. Far from it. There is no guilt attached to money, despite what fools may imply. If you acquire your money by robbing others, this is a different matter. Regardless of what thieves may think or say, their inner guilt is never appeased by donating some of their ill-gotten gains to those less fortunate. The same applies to those whose greed leads them to become "respectable" thieves.

Helping others is often a convenient conscience-reliever put forward by people who themselves seek more money. I have lost count of the number of letters I have read asking me how to solve money problems, while at the same time adding, almost as an afterthought, ". . . and help others." Guilt, pure guilt. Help others because you want to, not because you feel you have to.

The way to help others is by first helping yourself, not in any greedy, hoarding way, but by becoming a source of plenty. If you are content, this in itself will act as an example to others and, more to the point, you will be keeping money moving. Money that moves, circulates, and purchases, keeps people in employment, if nothing else. Also, if you feel the need to give (and there is nothing wrong with giving), then do it without guilt. Give purely for the joy of giving.

On the subject of giving, how many of you insist on paying for something that is offered free of charge or feel that you "owe" someone because they have done you a favor? If you are one of these people, stop and think, because you are making a big mistake. When somebody offers help or gives something to you, unless they ask for something in return, there is no debt incurred. So why insist on being indebted? By all means, give thanks, friendship, love, or any positive quality that is within your capability to give. But never chain yourself to a debt that does not exist. In any case, if you persist, people will eventually stop giving. Why? Because you are, in a way, insulting them. They wish to give freely. You are rejecting this by insisting on repaying a nonexistent debt. Accept gifts no matter how great or small. Realize that people need to give, because this gives them pleasure. Thank them, because they are both friendly and creative—even if the gift is unwanted. After all, you can always give it to someone else who may need it more than you do. I should point out that I am not implying that you should take all that is given to you and only give away the items that you do not want. Far from it. To give is part of the art of gaining. What I am saying is that you should give, by all means. But give from the heart, not out of a sense of guilt or rejection.

The need to pay for everything is a sign of guilt and is based on feelings of unworthiness. It is not something that people do deliberately. It is an automatic response. In other words, habits are the result of beliefs—beliefs that have been inherited, rather than thought about. I have given you one such example. There are many more, each one giving rise to a problem that is likely to stand in the way of success. As stated previously, the secret of success lies, not only in acquiring power, but in ridding yourself of wrong ideas by unlearning them.

Attracting Money

You have the power to attract money into your life in perfectly natural ways. That power exists within you, so let your inner mind utilize this potential by relaxing, letting go, and allowing it to work. Trust your inner mind. Let it work for you. Bring your mind around to the idea of money, lots of money, in fact, heaps of it! Do not be specific at this stage. Instead, see money coming toward you, pouring through the mailbox, arriving by the truckload, so much that there is no place to store it. Do not dismiss this as some form of childish stunt. It is not. What you are doing is telling your inner mind that you need an abundant supply of money. Become involved in this imaginary exercise as though it were real—treat it as such in your imagination. In short, indulge yourself in this vision. You should not find it too difficult, especially if you are capable of indulging in worry, which is simply the reverse of what has just been described. If you can see a lack of money and imagine all sorts of horrors (which, incidentally, have probably not happened, because they are only fears rather than actualities), you can just as easily see an abundance of money. If you persist, this, in itself, will start to obliterate the effects of negative thinking. You are, therefore, bound to improve your general frame of mind, not to mention the effects on your inner mind, in terms of direct instruction.

The rule is to think about an aspect of money. Turn it over in your mind, with the aid of your imagination, and then put feeling and belief into the thought. What have you got to lose by trying this? The answer is, nothing. You do, however, have much to gain. If you really want a bigger bank balance, then "see" this in your mind as though it were real. Believe that it will be so, and it will!

One of the most popular ways to apparently solve money problems is by winning vast amounts of money in a contest or lottery. Thousands of people spend large amounts of time trying to do this, either hoping and wishing that this will come true or, in more direct action, through the purchase of "winning methods." Having failed miserably, many turn to the mysterious world of Magick and try their hand at "instant" magical formulas. Others buy lucky charms, usually by the handful. What a waste of time and money! Quite apart from the fact that they have been misled, they have narrowed down their perspective to only one avenue. Far better to think about what you really want, use creative visualization to instruct the inner mind, and then allow it to function in its own way along the best available channel. It will find this with ease if you trust it to do so. Narrowing down the channels by presuming that money must arrive in a certain way reduces your chances of success.

So far, you have been shown how to instruct your inner mind to increase your supply of money in a general way. When you are proficient with the general exercise, you may move on to specific problems or needs. Again, use relaxation, together with the idea of an abundant money supply, as described. Then turn your attention toward a specific need, such as an unpaid bill. Do not worry over this. Instead, simply imagine that it is paid. Also, do not concern yourself with how this will come about. Leave this to your inner mind. Instead, concentrate on seeing the bill paid in full, as though it were actually true. See it with the word "Paid" stamped on it. Try to feel the satisfaction of having this problem removed. In short, indulge yourself in this imaginary situation, keeping in mind that this is, in reality, a magical exercise designed to get results. Remember to think expansively. In this case, see yourself being in a position where you never have to concern yourself with unpaid bills.

Chapter 20

Wealth

As you now know, you have an inner mind of limitless power, enormous insight, and vast potential. Its soul purpose is to serve you, because it is part of you, part of the totality of your being. You cannot be separated from it, nor can you be denied it. Your inner mind has access to unrestricted memory and can therefore provide answers to any question. It is, likewise, connected to everything in existence, including the immense power of the tides of cosmic energy that constantly flow into the universe. By mediating this energy on your behalf, by using it according to your needs and desires, your inner mind has the capacity to manifest whatever you wish into your life. There are no limits. Nothing is impossible to your inner mind. Ask and it will be given. That is the law. Do not seek to be rational or to doubt. Instead, accept this simple truth of inner-mind power as a reality. In the past, those who have accepted this as reality have grown to know the truth and have discovered abundant power and potential.

You are now on your way to
having everything you really want.

Working for Wealth

Wealth is not merely money, it is an attitude of mind. A lack of wealth is, therefore, due to wrong attitudes and beliefs that act contrary to truth. There is no evil in being wealthy. Wealth is simply a means to an end. We use it to get what we need. If our needs are great, we need more wealth. Wealth creates employment and brings abundance into the lives of many. If your wealth is limited and inadequate, this is not due to bad luck, fate, or misfortune. It is entirely due to wrong attitudes of mind. Nor does any god or supposed supreme entity seek to deprive or torment you. This is not the way of cosmos. It is simply a wrong attitude of mind. Deep down within your inner mind are beliefs and attitudes which suggest to your inner mind that you desire "limited" funds and have no interest in wealth or self-betterment. These act as instructions that, with the full power of your inner mind, are brought into physical reality.

Fortunately, this need not continue, because your inner mind is always willing to improve matters and accept new instructions, regardless of what has gone before. Now is the time to instruct your inner mind to procure wealth and increase your resources in real terms. All you have to do is ask and it will be given. The fact that you have purchased this book shows that you desire wealth and that you are prepared to do something positive about it. You have already sown the seeds of wealth in your inner mind. Now you must turn those seeds into an abundant harvest.

Be realistic. Wealth does not fall from heaven or materialize out of thin air. Wealth must find its way to you along precise channels. Money does not constitute wealth. Wealth is different for each person. Therefore, when you ask your inner mind to seek wealth, allow it to find these channels in its own way. Do not wonder how or why this will be done. Trust your inner mind to do it and it will, for it has the ability to see around obstacles and find the most expedient way of bringing you wealth. Be patient; everything takes time. Your inner mind will find what is the right time for you, based on the best possible use of cosmic-energy flow.

The Wealth Exercise—Part 1

The Wealth Magick ritual exercise should be used in conjunction with the cosmic sphere and the four symbolic doorways as follows:

I desire and ask for abundant wealth to enable me to meet all expenses, pay all bills, and purchase all those things I need.

[Imagine that the eastern doorway opens. Use a command phrase, if desired, remembering that the eastern doorway is in front of you.]

I desire and ask for wealth and the wisdom to use it to my best advantage.

[Imagine that the southern doorway now opens.]

I desire and ask for good fortune and opportunities to increase my wealth.

[Imagine that the western doorway now opens.]

I desire and ask for an attitude of mind so that restrictive thoughts, habits, and beliefs are replaced by truth, thereby paving the way to wealth-consciousness.

[Imagine that the northern doorway now opens.]

From now on, trust your inner mind to bring this to you by natural means. Do not doubt, for there is nothing to be gained by this. Instead, be optimistic and enthusiastic, and expect results. Day by day, as you practice these techniques, your inner mind will respond in ways that will surprise you. Be content to trust your inner mind to achieve your desires and to find the channels in which these may be brought to fruition. Every time you perform this ritual, relax, safe in the knowledge that your inner mind is responding to your needs and is working on your behalf on unseen levels. Be content to allow this to happen.

Now it is the time to return to normal consciousness. To close the ritual, use a command phase to close doors, seeing this happen in your imagination. Then close down the cosmic sphere in the usual way.

Resolve to practice these techniques each day, as directed. Continuity is the secret to success, so grasp this opportunity to succeed by setting aside a period of each day in which to practice these techniques. By doing so, you will increase the impact on your inner mind and you will aid the energies of the universe to do their work on your behalf.

The Wealth Exercise—Part 2

As with the first part of this ritual, find a quiet place where you can practice. It will guide you to the limitless power and potential of your inner mind. Do not strain to see mental pictures or concern yourself in any way. The more you relax, the better the result.

Wealth is an attitude of mind. As you think, so you are. And as you practice these techniques and relax, so your attitude toward wealth will change. As it changes, so will your circumstances. Wealth is not for the gifted few; any one can be wealthy. It is all a question of your attitude toward wealth. Wealth is not governed by fate or luck, nor is it dispensed by some remote god to those who are apparently favored. These are wrong attitudes of mind, wrong beliefs. You can be wealthy, you can have whatever you wish from life—not by sheer hard work, but by allowing these things to happen. Remember that word—*allow*.

Until now, you have allowed wrong thinking to dominate your life by accepting thoughts of restriction and need. These thoughts have been adopted, in turn, by your inner mind and so have become fact. Matters can so easily be changed by giving new instructions to your inner mind, which, with undying faith, will act on these to produce remarkable changes. Wealth can so easily be yours by simply changing your thoughts.

All around you is abundant energy, life-force. It is abundant and never-ending. Within the totality of this vast supply of cosmic power is the energy that is specific to life. This energy, this power, must exist, otherwise no one would ever be wealthy. There is an energy force for everything in existence. Therefore, anything is possible if we allow these energies to work for us instead of assuming the worst. The energy that manifests wealth exists here and now. It is all around you, waiting to be directed. Until now, you have used this energy to produce the opposite effect by believing that wealth is beyond you. The power simply conformed to your beliefs.

Now read the absolute truth!

If you are experiencing a lack of wealth, a lack of opportunity, unhappiness or troubles, it is because you are misusing power. If you have the power to manifest restriction, then you must have the power to manifest wealth. It is the same power, the same energy. Do not blame others, do not even blame yourself. Instead, realize that problems are caused by using wealth-energy in the wrong way. Realize that this power responds to what is expected of it. Realize that, if you can cause need, you can just as easily cause abundance. All it takes is to adopt more realistic beliefs. From then on, this power will proceed to manifest abundance in surprising ways.

The more you practice these techniques with an open mind, the more easily you will attract wealth. The more you allow these simple truths to enter your mind, the quicker will be the result. Wealth can so easily be yours by allowing that truth into your mind. From now on, wealth is about to pour into your life, provided that you practice the techniques and absorb the ideas. Believe the ideas given to you and you will know abundance, wealth, and happiness, for this is your right, regardless of what has happened in the past. Follow me now, as I lead you to the center of your own power, where dreams become reality and wishes come true.

A Wealth Ritual

Here is a "master ritual" that can be used for acquiring all your needs and desires. It requires a good deal of practice to make it work. Naturally, you do not need to use all of these suggestions, or even these same words. It is more important that you make individual choices. Change or modify whatever you wish, but remember that this process should be used at least once every day, and as many additional times as you wish. It is most effective first thing in the morning and last thing at night. The basic format follows.

1. Open the ritual by using the cosmic sphere of the three rings.

2. Enter the inner temple. In the initial stages, this consists of the four doorways and the central pool. Walk inside the inner temple, you are now in an enormous hall. In the center of this hall is a pool. Walk slowly toward it. You are now standing right in front of the pool. The pool glows with power and shines with light. Allow this power to work for you. Do not disbelieve; do not doubt. Let the power work for you by sinking your needs and desires into the pool. Allow it to bring wealth, success, and untold happiness into your life. Once your needs and desires, or your intention, has been put into this energy, it changes from a static, placid pool into a fountain of energy literally pulsating with power.

3. Perform the main work, which consists of reading your list of intentions as prepared in their positive, accomplished form (see page 93). It is essential that the visualized wish and affirmation be carried out completely and in the most effective way.

Let me give you an example of two properly worded desires and the proper way to affirm them. One is a desire concerning a materialization of a physical reality, the other a personal quality. We start with the need for $200 to pay an overdue debt and the wish to stop smoking. Correctly stated, these wishes become the following goals: "The $200 bill from the East Midland Electric Company is paid in full" and "I do not smoke. I do not waste my money on smoking cigarettes, cigars, or a pipe."

When affirming your daily needs and desires, read the first one aloud. Then visualize the bill in question with "Paid in

Full" stamped across it. If the bill itself is in your possession, take it in hand, examine it, and state the desire again. Then turn the bill face down and state the desire again, aloud.

Then read the second goal aloud, giving thought to the exact meaning of each word. You should visualize a situation in which that quality—no smoking—might be important (when buying tobacco in a shop, or when offered a smoke by a friend). Now visualize the situation as you would like it to occur. The visualization will present the correct image to the inner mind. Then, when you are faced with the real situation, you will have this positive material to draw on, rather than the failures that were the only information available before.

This pattern should be followed for every need and desire. The use of affirmations is absolutely essential to your successful practice of creative visualization. Read each need and desire aloud, if at all possible. If this cannot be done, move your lips and form the words silently as you read. After you have affirmed each need and desire, pause, then visualize it completely in the fountain. In your mind's eye, see the car, the home, the office with your name on the door. Touch the steering wheel, walk through the door. Feel the money from the first paycheck in your hands in cash. Count it, see each bill and know its denomination. You have now accepted the power of wealth and, from now on, it must manifest in your life. How will you spend this wealth? What will you do with it? Be positive and open-minded, realizing that all is possible if you keep faith with the power.

All around you is power, power to bring wealth into your life, power that will respond to your will. You can attract wealth, more wealth than you can ever use. It will never run out. It is yours. It is pouring into your life. Do not doubt. Accept this gift, for it is rightfully yours! Hold out your hands and welcome wealth into your life. The doorway of opportunity is also opening. People will become more favorably inclined toward you. They will be far more helpful, they will want to know you, they will want to help you succeed in life.

Let them do this. Grasp any offer that will help you succeed, because it is being given freely by those who now truly wish to give. All around you, the power will be working on unseen levels, bringing wealth into your life. All you have to do is keep faith with the power by dwelling on those things you wish to achieve. Know that a pure sustained thought or desire, backed up by persistent creative visualization, will eventually get results.

4. After visualizing your needs and desires amid the energy of the fountain, see this power pour out of the cosmic sphere though those four doorways into the outside world. Now it is time to leave. Close down the four gateways. In front of you is a doorway. Pass through it and see and feel yourself leaving the inner temple. Then close down the cosmic sphere and return to your own place and time. These procedures can be enhanced by using music, incense, and a self candle, if so desired.

You have read the truth and have been given a model for instructing your inner mind to bring this into your life. It will do this, but you can help by practicing these techniques regularly. Do not make excuses to yourself that you do not have the time. Make time. Surely this is worth the effort. Do not be put off. Determine to succeed, regardless of what appears to be happening at the moment. You can and will succeed, if you keep faith with power and truth. Whenever you have spare time, think about what you want from life, dream a little, expand your horizons. What are you going to do with this money? How are you going to use this newfound wealth? Go into the silence of your mind. Erect the cosmic sphere and think about your needs and desires. Let your imagination work in the widest possible sense. For with this wealth, anything is possible.

What will you do now? How will your life change for the better? Imagine what you can do and have: a new car, a bigger house, a business of your own, expensive cloths, and regular vacations. By doing this, you will be giving the power channels along which to flow and you will be speeding up the process of wealth-consciousness and ultimate fulfillment. Wealth can be yours, but it is proportional to your efforts. The more you put in, the more you get out! So perform these techniques regularly and allow wealth to find you. It is my sincere desire that you discover the power of the inner mind and its ability to manifest wealth. All I ask is that you help me to help you by practicing these ideas. Build them into a belief system and thereby allow power and truth to replace previous unsatisfactory conditions. I am confident that you will succeed.

Chapter 21

Love

If there were such a thing as a Top-Ten list of human desires, money, better health, and love would compete for first place. In fact the present esoteric market seems to be obsessed with selling books and goods that are supposed to cure all these too frequent problems. In this chapter, we will look at creative visualizations concerned with love and personal relationships.

There appear to be two different approaches to bringing love into your life: charms and talismans, and do-it-yourself kits or books of "guaranteed" spells. In the first instance, a lucky charm is likely to be a complete waste of time and money. These things are sold by the thousand to unsuspecting and gullible people who seek an easy way out of the dilemma of loneliness and lack of suitable companionship. I have to go on record by saying that I have no knowledge of a lucky charm that ever brought lasting happiness to anyone. Talismans, if correctly made (and this is rare!), can produce the results you desire, but much depends on that desire, as you will see. When things are clear in your mind (and it is hoped that this book will assist you in this), if you still think that a talisman is the answer, you can purchase one from a reputable talismanic worker, one of those few people who create talismans especially designed for individuals. So-called ancient designs are, I assure you, not guaranteed to bring success. In any case, unless these things are ritually enhanced, using correct magical techniques, they will prove to be just as useless as the aforementioned lucky charms.

With regard to do-it-yourself kits, much depends on the contents, but especially on the abilities of the person who intends to use these things. In short, if you are not fully conversant with meaningful magical practices, you will again be wasting your time and money. In all fairness, your magical supplier simply has no idea whether or not you are capable. They have to assume that, when you purchase something, you do indeed know what you are doing. It is another matter, however, to knowingly sell supposedly guaranteed spell kits that are filled with the most ludicrous nonsense imaginable. This is unethical, unkind, and disturbing, to say the least. Perhaps the worst offenders, when it comes to peddling misinformation, are those people who tell you how to command other souls to fall under your spell. This is the height of stupidity and can only be classified as absolute and utter rubbish. Once, and for all time, let me set the record straight. If—and it is a big "if"—you are talented or lucky enough to compel someone to do something against his or her "true will," you will, at best, score only a temporary victory. Sooner or later, that "true will" is bound to reverse the situation and you, as the perpetrator of this crime, will then be faced with the consequences of your actions, whatever these may be. Never try to influence others by using commands. You will be asking for trouble, in addition to causing unnecessary problems for someone else.

The one and only time that you can influence someone else is when they truly wish to respond to your wishes. Do avoid these silly ideas that put money into pockets of idiots and leave you with an even greater problem than you had before. The correct way to secure real and lasting relationships is to look very carefully at the real problem—*you*. Please do not think that I am being harsh or trying to undermine your self-confidence. I assure you that I am not. All that I truly wish for anyone who has this sort of problem is that they find a lasting and realistic solution. Remember the truest words ever spoken: "As you think, so you are." In other words, your dominant thoughts will always dictate what happens to you throughout this earthly life. This is due to the fact that all dominant thoughts affect the inner mind and, as you now know, the inner mind will always respond to these thoughts, because they are beliefs. If you are lonely, it is because you are projecting this thought pattern out toward other people. Probably not consciously, but unconsciously, without knowing it. You, like everyone else, act just like the pole of a magnet. You can attract or you can repel. In order to change things, you must change your polarity so that it produces much more favorable results.

Take a long look at yourself and be perfectly honest. This is the vital first step in putting things right. Look at your physical appearance, for so often the outer shell is a reflection of the inner being. Are you projecting a happy, confident image, or are you down in the dumps, having effectively given up? Look at what you are and what you have. Are you making the best use of this or not? Are you being yourself or are you a poor reflection of what others think you should be? From the opposite point of view, do not be put off if you do not have film-star looks or a large bank balance. What really matters is you. If you are not being you, then you are not projecting the right image. Even the most portly, balding person has something to offer. All they have to do is to find this and this means looking for it. So look at yourself. Discard your more negative parts and bolster your more positive attributes. This is not difficult, but it does take some effort and a willingness to accept the truth, however this may appear at first sight. If you do not think much of yourself, how can you expect someone else to like you? As you think, so you are. Change this thinking and you most certainly will change your circumstances.

To sum up the first step to getting things on a better footing, look at yourself, be honest with yourself and, above all else, look at the way in which you think. If you are constantly putting yourself down, hiding away from life, or projecting thoughts that repel others (thoughts such as, "Please go away, I am too shy to talk to you"), you are not likely to meet with any degree of success, no matter how much money you spend on books and charms. Get your thinking right and all else will soon fall into place.

The Mirror Exercise

A very useful exercise can be performed with an ordinary mirror. Sit down and look at yourself. I mean really *look* and *think* about you. Are you too shy, filled with apprehension, or are you completely egotistical? Do not be afraid to face yourself. Remember that everyone has problems, so you are not alone. Spend as long as you like on this, for it is a valuable exercise.

Now write down a list of all your faults and all your good points. This is extremely valuable, because it gets these things up to the surface. Then make a list of all those things you would really like to be. Again, do not imitate others. This serves no useful purpose. At best, it means that you wish to be a poor reflection of someone else. The truth of the matter is that you will only be truly happy when you discover who you really are and what you are capable of. The human mind can achieve anything, if it is used properly. The exercises given previously will help in preparing you to use your mind—your inner mind—in a powerful, yet natural, way.

The next stage involves the imagination. This takes only a few minutes each day, but should be a regular practice if you truly wish for success. By far, one of the biggest causes of failure in creative visualization is the lack of persistence. If you want something, be prepared to put some effort into it. Find somewhere quiet. Sit down and relax, clearing your mind of all doubts, worries, and uncertainties. If you have carried out the instructions given previously, you should have quite a lot of knowledge about yourself and should know the type of person you really want to be. Think about this person, the new you. In your imagination, see yourself as that person: confident, attractive, calm, and self-assured. Do this with your eyes open or closed. It makes no difference. Feel yourself being this new person, act it out in your mind, or, to use a childlike term, pretend. There is nothing wrong with pretense, if it is used as a creative tool like this. Be this person, live the image and feel good about it. Practice this as often as you like, but do it at least once each day for as long as it takes to get in the right mood.

Those of you who bought this book hoping to hear of powerful magical rituals, words of power, and specialized equipment may be a little disappointed by now. This, after all, is a book devoted to "shaping reality"—in other words, creative visualization techniques that are supposed to get results. Well, dear reader, this *is* a book on creative visualization—*real* creative visualization. For creative visualization is the science of using the mind and it is my job to teach you how to do this. Forget about magical and self-help stereotypes, the supposed words of power, guaranteed equipment, and proven spells. These belong either in the Dark Age or on the refuse heap.

There is a use for ritual words and equipment. They can help focus the mind, but they are only of use if you use the mind correctly and if they are relevant to the task at hand. Learn to use your mind first, then use whatever other means are available to help you concentrate along the lines being worked. With regard to love, the correct energy is that which corresponds to the planet Venus. Leave aside superstition and those copious lists of attributions, god-names, and unrealistic symbols. It is far better to keep things simple and only use those correspondences that matter. In the case of Venus, we are dealing with the color green. This may be worked into the ritual in many ways (candles, altar cloths), if this seems reasonable to you. Use a good-quality venusian incense. By good quality, I mean one that has been specifically made by someone who knows what they are doing. Remember that it is not the equipment that gets results, it is the power that lies within you—in your mind. These things are simply there to help you focus your mind along the right channel of energy, in this case Venus.

Also, do not, for heaven's sake, make the mistake of thinking that you are dealing with the planet Venus as such. This is nonsense, for the physical planet has no effect whatsoever on human affairs. Venus is a symbol, nothing more. As for the gods and those highly dubious god-names, there are no gods. You are not dealing with some far-removed being on the outer reaches of the galaxy or in some other state of existence. You are dealing with energy, natural energy—in this case, the energy that conforms to the essential idea of Venus, attraction and love. No god stands in your way, nor do you have to fall on your knees before it or any of its supposed angels. People or books that tell you to do this sort of thing should be laughed at rather than listened to. The idea of gods and superpowers are a corruption of the art of using personalized symbols or telesmatic images. Unless you understand these techniques, it is far better to leave well-enough alone.

Here is a useful creative visualization designed to bring love into your life in a meaningful and lasting way. If you have a particular person in mind, well and good. But do remember what has already been said about commanding or compelling other people. If you wish to attract in truth, then you will have to build in certain safeguards. This is quite easy. First, set up your altar using the ideas already given. The choice of equipment, candles, and other items is entirely up to you, so do think about this carefully. See which things appeal to you the most and work accordingly. The only imperative in any creative visualization procedure is that you must have peace and quiet and somewhere where you will not be disturbed. Trying to work creative visualization with half your mind on the probability of being disturbed is likely to be unfruitful. You need to be able to relax, both before and during creative visualization.

At the appointed time, relax and clear your mind, then construct the cosmic sphere. Use the four gateways, if you wish. After opening all the gateways, face the northern gate that corresponds to Venus. All this, of course, can be performed as a seated meditation. Now imagine that a bright green light is building up within your heart. See it getting brighter, then see it growing, until it covers you completely. Imagine that you are now a magnet, pulling in useful relationships, social engagements, and companionship.

You can burn some good-quality venusian incense and light a green candle to represent the power of the planetary energy. Immediately behind the candle, see in your imagination a green doorway that opens, letting in even more green light.

See this fill your room. Continue to feel yourself attracting people as described. Do this for as long as you like. To close the exercise, see the doorway close, then see the light fade away. Extinguish your altar candle. You should perform this creative visualization over a period of time, perhaps once a day for a month. It is also advisable to continue with the use of the imaginary exercises given previously, as this helps to maintain positive thinking and keeps negative thinking at bay.

If your creative visualization intention is to bring a specific person into your life, you will need to invoke a safeguard. At the point where you see the door open, simply imagine that the other person walks through that door and stands in front of you. Imagine that you hold out your hands and that the other person does the same. Gently, your hands touch and a great warmth flows through you both. There is no compulsion, no coercion, no commands. Just love and friendship. This is an equal partnership involving complete give and take. Each of you is free to do and think as you please. At closing, this other person simply leaves through the door, which then closes behind them.

When performed this way, this exercise involves no risk. Sooner or later you will either succeed or you will learn why this may not be. In either case, you are successful, if you care to think about it. For there is nothing to be gained by trying to enslave someone. Read this chapter many times and practice the principles given, because they do work, although often in surprising ways. If nothing else, it will save you a lot of money that might have been wasted on unrealistic ventures.

Chapter 22

Healing

What exactly do we mean by healing? Quite simply, healing may be defined as the restoration of a desired status quo—in other words, going back to whatever existed prior to an illness. Healing, therefore, equates to balance. When someone is ill or incapacitated, the balance has been disturbed. With illness, a person is uncomfortable, ill at ease. In fact, the word "disease," or "dis-ease," shows this to be true. There are, of course, many forms of healing, from conventional medicine to the "laying on of hands," as it is called. It is not the purpose of this part of the book to discuss the merits or failings of conventional medicine. These are too well-known to need further discussion. However, I cannot condone the actions of certain drug companies and those who prescribe dangerous chemicals without a second thought. Often, these things cause more harm than good—particularly tranquilizers and sedatives. With most drugs, the rule now seems to be that today's wonder drugs bring tomorrow's side effects.

Having said this, it is always a good idea to see your medical practitioner in serious cases of ill health or uncertainty. Your general practitioner ought to be given the opportunity to diagnose your illness. For mild aliments, or the supposedly incurable illnesses that have been written off by modern science, magical healing is often the answer. Creative visualization also forms the basis of positive-thought training, used to promote health. Carl and Stephanie Simonton use these autosuggestive techniques in their Texas-based visualization therapy. In this therapy, patients vividly fantasize that diseased cells are being destroyed and dispersed, for example, by a regiment of soldiers. It is all a question of choice and the application of common sense. After all, there is no need to bother your doctor with a slight cold, nor is there any need to perform a full-scale ritual. You can just as easily take a harmless herbal potion.

Quite a lot of illnesses are due to a person's state of mind. Fear, worry, anxiety, and depression can all take their toll. There is a lot to be said for keeping your body healthy and reasonably fit, but there is an even greater case to be made for encouraging people to acquire healthy minds. Someone who is naturally optimistic and cheerful is generally less likely to become ill. Indeed, more and more medical practitioners are arriving at the idea that quite a lot of illnesses are psychosomatic—in other words, exist only in the mind. Belief patterns govern life, and they also govern health. The lesson is thus: Think healthy, and you will be healthy. Prevention is better than cure, especially today, when mental stress is at an all-time high. Stress and tension injure the body and make it more receptive to both negative thinking and disease. The mind is a powerful instrument, and stress can make it work the wrong way. It therefore becomes necessary to organize your thinking into a healthy pattern, by adopting stress-reducing techniques, together with regular sessions of clearing the mind of toxins.

The world teaches us to rush, to panic, to sweat and strain, to fight every inch of the way. Little wonder that people suffer breakdowns, for this is not the way of nature. Look at nature, for it has much to teach us about life. There is no rush there, only peace. And peace is the way to health. After all, if you are in a stressed condition, you are given tranquilizers to calm you, to make you slow down and rest. Far better to use the principle of peace in a more natural way. Seek nature's help. Go out into the fresh air—not in a city, for these places are psychic vacuums, generally devoid of vital energy or Earth currents. Listen to the sounds of nature and look at the gentle colors. These things are worth far more than all the drugs in the world. Learn tranquillity and peace in your own home by taking control of your mind, by slowing down, by resting it, and by clearing it of unwanted thoughts and worries. Make this a new habit and it will repay you many times over. There is no need to take up yoga, for those positions are quite meaningless to a Western mind, even if they do tone up the muscles. A nice walk in the fresh air will do just as much good. Take up the practice of relaxation. By this, I do not mean lying around watching TV. I mean the *art* of relaxation, of deliberately letting go of every muscle until you are completely relaxed. Then go on to relax your mind, which can be a much more difficult thing to do. Good music and incense can help with this. Try bringing your mind some pleasant scene or event from the past. Alternatively, imagine that you are in some ideal location, like a far-away island or country cottage. Sessions like this can do wonders for your mind and your general health.

Here is a simple creative ritual that can be used to heal you or others. It uses the energy of the Sun, so you must work this into your ritual, using any objects that remind you of solar power (for instance, a gold- or yellow-colored altar cloth, with similarly colored candles). The incense should be frankincense, or any good-quality solar incense. Start by laying out your altar and preparing your workroom. You will need three candles. Two should be in gold or yellow. The remaining candle represents the person being healed. This can be plain white or, better still, it can be colored to suit the person in need of healing. There are many ways of determining this. Perhaps the best way is to use the color that equates to a person's birth sign. These are given in Table 3 (see page 164).

Before starting, you should keep these facts in mind:

1. You cannot perform effective visualization with the necessary concentration if you are likely to be disturbed. You simply will not be able to relax fully if half your mind is concerned with the probability of somebody barging in on you. Take steps to see that you will not be disturbed.

2. The timing of this ritual is not critical. In fact, you can do it any time. Forget about those ludicrous days of the week given in certain publications. Without going into detail, suffice it to

Table 3. Birth Signs and Their Corresponding Colors.

SIGN	COLOR	SIGN	COLOR
Aries	Red	Libra	Emerald Green
Taurus	Orange-Red	Scorpio	Turquoise Blue
Gemini	Orange	Sagittarius	Deep Blue
Cancer	Amber or Silver	Capricorn	Purple
Leo	Yellow or Gold	Aquarius	Violet
Virgo	Light Green	Pisces	Cardinal Red/Crimson

say that these are nonsense. Simple common sense tells you that it is silly to assume that solar energy can only work on a Sunday.

3. Creative visualization works through the power of your inner mind and your ability to influence this part of yourself. There are no gods or entities to which you appeal. You deal with power directly.

4. Before the ritual, clear your mind of everyday thoughts. Calm down and become tranquil, as this is the only way power can be contacted.

5. To succeed, it is vital that you think positively. It is simply no use hoping and wishing that you may perhaps be successful. This is the wrong approach. Be assertive and believe that you will be successful. Positive thinking always gets positive results, and perhaps the great cause of failure is negative thinking. Be realistic. You cannot expect your inner mind to respond to your wishes if you are, on the one hand, asking it to heal, while, on the other hand, you are filled with doubts and uncertainties.

Any ritual should have a symbolic basis. This is quite easily accomplished by using the master symbol of the encircled cross. Start by relaxing and imagining that you are standing in a magical circle, a cosmic circle of golden light—the cosmic sphere.

In front of you is the magical point of east and a yellow doorway; to your right is the magical point of south and a red doorway; behind you is the magical point of west and a blue doorway; to your left lies the magical point of north and a green doorway. From where you stand in the center, paths reach out to each of the four doorways. As they do, the doors open slowly, revealing the four magical weapons. In the east is a magical sword; in the south is a magical wand; in the west is a magical silver chalice; in the north is a circular magical shield. Approach the altar and light the two gold candles that are placed there, about twelve inches apart. These two lights represent the pillars that stand on either side of another door. Imagine that this secret doorway actually exists and that it is opening slowly to reveal an altar in the shape of a cube. This altar glows with golden light and radiates peace and harmony. It is the altar of the Sun. Remember that, although this is seen in your imagination, it is nevertheless a powerful symbol.

Light the candle that represents the person to be healed. This should be placed between the two gold candles. Turn your attention back to the solid-gold cubic altar and imagine that the person to be healed is now standing behind it. Continuing to use your imagination, take the central candle and give it to this person. As you do, they are covered in brilliant golden light. Spend at least five minutes concentrating on this person, seeing all light driving out illness, disease, and stress. To close the exercise, extinguish the central candle, see the doorway close, and watch it fade away. Extinguish the two gold candles. Finally, turn your attention to the four magical points once more, and starting in the east and working in a clockwise direction, see each door close and fade away. Finally, see the cosmic sphere disappear.

This ritual uses very little equipment, for equipment is not the key to success. Real Magick is done in your mind, in your imagination. Note that you do not have to visualize as such. To imagine something is far easier, and this can be done with your eyes open or closed. For those not familiar with the techniques of imaginary creative visualization, I remind you that these are fully covered in chapter 6 of this book.

Chapter 23

Power

This creative visualization exercise is designed to put real power at your disposal in a safe and natural way. The practical work that follows will be of enormous value to you, no matter what your path or persuasion.

The practical work presented here is particularly valuable to all who wish for better things, yet have limited time and equipment. It is based on a technique that I have used and have given to friends and others over the years. Originally, it was intended as a preritual exercise, but I have now modified it for everyday use. It lasts only five or ten minutes and should be done at least once a day, preferably first thing in the morning. You will need no equipment, only somewhere quiet in which to practice. You may, of course, elaborate on this as much as you like. Soft meditation music and incense are always useful tools.

Start by sitting comfortably and relaxing, gradually stilling your mind and pushing aside all thoughts of everyday matters. The more you relax, the better the results. It is often easier to cast your mind over something pleasant, a vacation, some ideal place, or some situation that appeals to you. When you are calm, with your eyes either open or closed, construct the cosmic sphere. Imagine that you are floating in the center of a large glasslike sphere. No need to strain to "visualize" this. Just imagine that it exists. Pretend, if you like. In front of you is a magical sword pointing upward. To your right is a magical spear pointing upward, glowing with bright light. Immediately behind you is a drinking horn or magic chalice, filled to overflowing with a pleasant blue liquid. To your left is a circular, black magical shield with a white equal-armed cross in the center. Above your head is a gold crown. Below you is the Earth itself, blue and green, covered with patches of pure white clouds.

Let your mind wander slowly over the vastness of space and the universe. Think about the enormous forces at work, in the Sun and in the stars. Realize that this is not chaotic. There is order, balance, and perfection. Behind all of this, there is a form of intelligence that creates order, and you are a part of that intelligence. You can name this God, the Logos, the Universal Mind, the Creative Source, the Demiurge, or whatever you like. It exists, and it exists for your benefit. That which created you will never harm you. It is a totally beneficial and absolute power. All you have to do is allow this power into your life and not in a subservient way or in fear. You do not have to sacrifice anything or put yourself at a disadvantage. You are allowing life-force and wisdom into your life. By opening up this channel to the infinite, you are contacting not only beneficence, but a higher part of yourself, that part of yourself that desires only the very best for you. Relax more deeply and let go.

Look toward the magical sword and say:

This day I desire freedom from stress, I desire peace of mind and clear thinking.

[There is no need to say this out loud. Just say it in your mind and mean it. Do not have doubts or fears. Say it as though you were speaking to someone who can and will help. For in truth, you are. Now look toward the magical spear and say:]

This day I desire energy, strength, vitality, and well-being.

[Once again, say it with conviction. Look toward the magical cup in your imagination and say:]

This day do I desire emotional fulfillment, tranquillity, optimism, and the opportunity to be happy and successful.

[Look toward the magical shield in your imagination once more and say:]

This day do I strongly desire all the good things of life, material abundance and satisfaction.

[Now relax and allow universal beneficence to come quietly into your life. There is no need to beg or implore. This is not the way of things. This power is yours. It is poised, ready to work wonders in all areas of your life. All you have to do is allow it to enter, if only for a few seconds. Let go, relax, and allow it into your life. That is all you have to do.]

To close the exercise, simply close down and imagine that the sphere has disappeared. Stretch your arms and legs and return to normal.

If you really want to let magical power change your life, this exercise is extremely valuable and it does not take up a lot of time. Do it every day. Gradually, you will notice a change, not only in yourself, but in other people and in your everyday life. By using inner guidance and power like this, you are bound to feel better and it is inevitable that you will be led toward fulfillment and happiness in natural ways. The choice is yours. Persist, and you are bound to gain on all levels of life.

Chapter 24

Protection

What do you do if a psychic attack comes your way or if you are in need of protection from aggression? How can you defend yourself? And how do you know for certain that you are under actual psychic attack? The last question is more important than the others, for, all too often, people allow their most powerful tool, the imagination, to run amok. Before you leap to the conclusion that you are under psychic attack, you must ask the following questions:

1. Exactly what is "wrong"? Make a list, if you have to. This often puts things into perspective. Then be honest. How much of this is due to perfectly normal occurrences? Also bear in mind that, if you are a negative thinker, chances are that you, and no one else, are responsible for your own misfortunes. The human mind can achieve literally anything, for better or for worse, and quite often, without realizing it, people are their worst enemies.

2. Exactly who is responsible? You must have upset someone in some way to cause them to do this sort of thing. There has to be a reason for psychic attack. To sustain the effort required to cause another human being harm takes a lot of "know how" and power. It is not a job for amateurs. The people who do specialize in this—and they do exist—also know about the laws of cause and effect. So they are not likely to bother you unless you really upset them, or they are being well paid. You must ask: "Am I truly worthy of such attention?" This sort of thing takes skill and expertise.

3. Are there any psychic phenomena bothering you? These may also be due to your own inherent psychism, which may be regrettably out of control. To avoid this, you should never "dabble" in Magick or psychic affairs. Get advice from a reputable magician, or a person well-versed in these matters and avoid spiritualism. Get your Magick or mind-power work onto a firm basis using sound techniques. Moreover, if you have not been involved in anything like this, please do not rush out and get exorcised. This is pointless. Seek advice from experts. They will help, usually without making any demands, and unless they have to spend money themselves, you will not be charged.

Most apparent psychic attacks are not psychic attacks at all. If you are unsure, ask yourself these questions first, then get advice if you need it. Should you ever be unfortunate enough to suffer direct interference from someone else, or have unresolved psychic problems, the following ritual will most certainly help to stabilize the situation until either the attacker runs out of steam, which they will, or the phenomenon recedes. Control is the keyword. You must control your thoughts and calm things down, for "chaos" is the intention. Also remember that your antagonist is using energy—the same sort of energy that every mind-power operator or magical practitioner uses. There is no difference, other than one of intention. So you need to employ control, calmness, and energy. Here is a way of using these to your advantage.

When you are absolutely certain that something is wrong, first find a quiet place. Then sit down and gradually gain control by breathing slowly in and out. Repeat to yourself often: "I am in control. I am calm." Feel yourself becoming calm and getting stronger. Take as long as you like with this. Remember that it is your opponent's time you are wasting, not yours. Give yourself the positive thought that you do not have to "accept" the energy directed at you. You can and will reject it utterly. Gradually, see in your imagination a spark of bright light within your heart that grows brighter and brighter, until it illuminates the entire room. See it pushing away all negative forces. This is not a silly exercise. It is very important and it does work. Hold this for as long as you like. Then connect yourself to the highest and mightiest force in the universe. Call it God, Divinity, the Universal Mind, or whatever you like, but realize and appreciate that no request made to this power is ever refused. It is your right to contact this power and you are entitled to help.

To do this, construct the cosmic sphere. See, in your imagination, a bright crown above your head, and a cube of solid black stone beneath your feet. In front of you is a shining sword. To your right is a blazing spear. Behind you is a chalice that overflows with power and goodness. To your left is a shield that cannot be penetrated. Hold these images in your mind. Believe that they are there because, in truth, they are. Now, imagine that you are surrounded by a fortress of solid stone (the inner temple). Nothing can get inside, unless you allow this to happen. Finally, use the gateways and pool. Ask for help; ask for power to defeat this attack. Do not be afraid and do not feel silly. Just ask with sincerity. Stay calm and expect help. It will come. After a while, you will notice that you are getting calmer and you will realize that it is over and that you are safe. This method works for a variety of reasons, too lengthy to discuss in this example. In brief, it works because you are employing control, correct symbology that invokes the imagination. And you are asking something of life itself, in a way that your inner mind understands.

If you wish to elaborate on this ritual, by all means do so. The stamp of individuality can only help. Construct your cosmic sphere, enter the inner temple, use the fountain, use candles (one for your inner light, the self candle, and four others to represent the sword, spear, chalice, and shield). As you see these visual images, light the appropriate candle. Imagine that your attacker is restrained in some way, perhaps in a jail house. If necessary, visualize the person in chains. Keep this person confined until they obey your wishes. Talk to the image as if it were a real person. Talk to it and tell it "what is what." You tell *them* what to do and how to do it. You order the person to make no opposition to your directions. Do not ask. *Order* them to obey. Then see them acting toward you in a friendly manner or following your commands. If the person is unknown to you, use a shadowy humanoid shape of some sort to represent the attacker. Use a little ingenuity, as it is your problem. And remember—never attack someone else, not even your assailant. You may be mistaken and this person may not be responsible. On the other hand, you are entitled to defend yourself against oppression like this. This ritual not only works for psychic attack, it also helps to clear unwanted psychic activity. This may never happen to you, but, in any case, it can do no harm to practice this ritual, looking on it rather as you would a fire drill.

Chapter 25

Career

This chapter is concerned with the ever-increasing problem of unemployment. On the surface, it seems as if the world is rapidly changing. New technology is moving in and millions of hardworking people are being sacrificed on the altar of progress. If you like, you can either give up and accept fate or bad luck, or be really negative and spend a lot of time and energy hating the establishment, the government, and everyone else who is even remotely connected with the problem. If you prefer these bad habits to a different reality, then so be it. But it really does not have to be like this at all.

The world changes constantly. Nothing lasts forever, nothing is really stable and secure in human life. Glance back at history. Did the architects of the Roman empire ever visualize its total collapse? Whatever happened to the Commonwealth, or to great civilizations like Egypt? Empires come and just as surely fade away. All is change; nothing ever remains static. The key to life and success is adaptability and a realization that nothing ever stands still. The law of nature is that you must adapt or perish, and so it is with all human affairs, from paupers to kings. No one can avoid the "wheel of change." The world is changing rapidly. We are entering a new era of great potential and, in keeping with the new dawn, there is always disruption, as old ideas and trends fade away, leaving the unadaptable behind. Many people willingly nail themselves to the cross of past habits, refusing to adapt and see the light. Like dinosaurs, they pass into history without having any effect on the future.

Even more pitiful are the confused ethics that drag us back to the old values and restore the old standards. They would take us back to the "good old days" that were nowhere near as good as they would have us believe. We can no more go back in time than we can live on mana. Our reality lies ahead, and we reach it by learning from the past, while at the same time allowing new ideas to bear fruit. It is important for those caught up in this confusion that they realize the truth behind the statement "the solution to every problem is within the problem itself." In reality, this is not a time for despair. It is a time for opportunity, if you make the effort. Never let apparent facts dictate how you must run your life. Stop! Think and make changes! In other words, adapt.

This part of the book is dedicated to those unfortunate individuals who have been temporarily pushed on to the scrap heap of change and are now unemployed, or in a very insecure position. You have a choice. You can look forward to early retirement or a life living off the state, or you can refuse to be pushed around and do something about it. For a start, do you really want to continue working in the same old job or something similar? Before you go out chasing vacancies or giving up altogether, stop and think. What is it that you really want to do? Just forget about earning a living and paying the bills, and ask yourself: What do you really want to do? Everyone has some talent, some special ability. The old idea that you must get any job in order to make ends meet or follow in the family footsteps is long dead. If you put your mind to work, you can end up, not only employed, but very happy and successful— more successful than you ever thought possible.

You must start by changing your thinking. You have some special talent that the world needs and wants. Do not dismiss this as nonsense. It is not. The economic framework of the world is not shaped by random factors. It is shaped by ideas. Once an idea is born, a market is automatically created along side it. Sometimes the idea is already there, but no one has seen its potential. If you think about what you really want to do, as opposed to accepting second best, you will automatically create a demand for your services. Time and time again, this has been written and has been proven true. So sit down and think, dream, and let your imagination work. Do not let "If only I had . . . ," or "If I were younger" thoughts get in the way. These are invalid arguments. When you think, you are giving power to your inner mind. As long as you are positive, you cannot fail.

One lady, who had reached the age of 100, emigrated to Australia to start a new life. Do you really want to write yourself off at 50? That's only half her age! Think about it! Age is no excuse. If you are only 25, then you *really* have no excuse. Perhaps you trained to become a mechanic and now no one wants to employ you. Do you really want to be a mechanic? Do you really love the job and enjoy every minute of it? Or did you take it because there was nothing around at the time and everyone else was into cars and bikes? It is time to think and decide what you really want. If you want to be a mechanic, well and good. If not, forget it and look somewhere else.

Here is a simple ritual that will help you to bring those new ideas into reality. All you need is three candles, somewhere quiet to work, and the determination to succeed. Your work space should have a flat surface that you can use as an altar. Cover it with a clean cloth. The choice of color is entirely up to you. Place a gold or yellow candle in the center of the altar. This represents the fruition of your desire. To the right, place a white candle to represent you; to the left, a black candle, to represent those people and energies who can help you in some way. You now have the magical "triplicity of power," represented as three pillars. Cabalistic thinkers will of course note that these also represent the three pillars on the Tree of Life.

The laws of creation work like this: There is a father force (white) that is directed to the receptive mother (black). The result is the magical child of light (gold). All creative processes work through this pattern—father, mother, child. This ritual is therefore based on sound magical practice and a symbolic pattern that your inner mind understands.

To perform this ritual, first spend time relaxing and clearing out everyday thoughts. This is most important. You cannot work effective rituals in a state of stress, desperation, or uncertainty.

Construct the cosmic sphere, then calm down and convince yourself that your inner mind will accept the ideas you present to it within the symbolic framework you are now about to erect. Take your time. When you are ready, see in your imagination a triangle of gold, pointing down, that appears immediately above the three candles. Its apex touches the central gold candle. You do not have to visualize or concentrate—the briefest glimpse will do. As long as you know that this now exists in your imagination, that is all that matters. Spend a few minutes knowing. Then light the white candle and think about yourself and the job you have in mind. Be positive and assertive. Spend a few minutes on this and then light the black candle. This time, feel that you are getting help in unseen ways and that everything and everybody is being cooperative. Reflect on this for a few minutes. Finally, light the central gold candle and spend a few minutes seeing yourself being successful and happy. Know that this is about to happen in its own way. To close, extinguish the candles and put everything away in a safe place.

A single ritual can go a long way toward helping achieve results, but it is far better to perform this over a period of time. Either perform this ritual every day for a week, or, if you prefer, once a week for a month. Once you start, do not be tempted to miss a ritual because you are too tired or do not feel like it. Unless you exert some effort now, you cannot reasonably expect success later. Think first, ritualize your thoughts, then persist, not only with the ritual, but with some more regular sessions of positive creative visualization similar to the ones described in previous chapters.

During the coming week, I recommend that you follow the directions given for the proper method of creative visualization and test for yourself its efficiency. As you have come to learn, the creative power within you is capable of bringing about a materialization of your innermost desires. Use it to obtain the career or job you would most like to have. Never accept second best.

Chapter 26

Problem Solving

What is meditation? What does it do? What is its real value? I will try to answer these questions and point the way to realistic meditational practices. Meditation is nothing more than a technique for gaining access to hidden levels of the inner mind. Meditation has much to offer, provided we use it properly. To do this, we must first remove any idea that is a mysterious process. Anyone can meditate and, with the right basis, you can teach yourself. Let us now look at the right basis.

Meditation is simply the ability to use your inner mind in a rather special way. Remember this: Your inner mind is your own miracle center, the "God within." Quite apart from its abilities to manipulate life's energies on your behalf, it also has limitless memory. In fact, it is true to say that every thought, every experience, everything that has ever happened, is stored within your inner mind.

Within the memory of your inner mind are the answers to all questions. All you have to do is gain access to them by using your mind in a certain way. Meditation has become something of a ritual and, although there is nothing wrong with ritual as such, matters have tended to go too far. To meditate successfully requires that you begin with a calm mind and that you are reasonably relaxed. So anything you can do to aid this is obviously worthwhile. Find somewhere quiet that is free from distractions, such as noise or, of course, other people not of a like mind. Anything you can do to create a peaceful atmosphere is also useful. Dimming the lights, playing soft music, lighting incense, or wearing loose clothing can all help to promote tranquillity. You do not need a special meditation robe. Wear whatever feels comfortable and helps promote calm and relaxation.

A Model for Meditation

Meditation should be done seated comfortably, hands resting on your lap. Sit down, get comfortable, and start to relax, then construct the cosmic sphere

Your first task is to control, or rather ignore, your conscious mind—in other words, your own thoughts. This is simple. There are several ways to do this, all based on the fact that you cannot think of two things at the same time. Try it! You cannot! So, if you are busy concentrating on something other than mundane affairs, your mind cannot be occupied with everyday matters. One technique is to concentrate on your breathing. Slow this down to an even and steady rate, and listen to each breath. It does not matter if you do this with your eyes open or closed. As you breathe in, listen and realize that you are taking in energy and life-force. As you breathe out, realize you are expelling unwanted products. Then take this one stage further, by continuing to overlay a pattern of thinking. Breathing in brings power, breathing out lets tension go and relaxes you. Breathe in power, breathe out tension—let go. Do this until you begin to feel calm and peaceful.

Now, stop concentrating on your breathing. In fact, let this continue in its own way, but keep your mind on the idea of the twofold process. Think about this, not forcefully, but gently, letting ideas arise quite naturally. Let me give you an example. As you breathe in, you take in oxygen. This is passed into the bloodstream and is carried by the blood to every part of your body. Your in-breaths keep you alive. By breathing in, you are taking in power and life-energy. Your out-breaths expel carbon dioxide. They get rid of unwanted waste products that can adversely affect your body. Both inhalation and exhalation are therefore necessary. Power in, waste out. Yet nothing is ever wasted, because nature uses these waste products and converts them back to useable commodities. There is a constant cycle, a harmonious balance. Let your mind become more deeply involved in this idea, without strain, without any real effort.

This is the way to learn meditation, by gradually bringing your mind to bear on a specific idea and then letting associated ideas arise quite naturally out of your inner mind. If your conscious mind starts to wander, which it often does in the initial stages, gently bring it back on target. With practice, you will find this is easy to do and, eventually, your mind will cease to wander altogether. You may wonder, "What is the point in all of this?" Well, there are several benefits. To begin with, meditation causes you to relax and so has tremendous benefits for your health. Try it for yourself and you will see. People simply do not realize that the mind is a tool. Think of it this way. If you wish to become strong, you exercise your muscles, you undergo a program of training. No one in their right mind would expect to become fit, or run the four-minute mile, without training. Likewise, if you wish to learn a musical instrument, you must study and practice. So it is with the mind. If you wish to gain the obvious benefits that these techniques can bestow, you must train your mind. You must exercise and control it.

Meditation helps achieve this control and a controlled mind will produce enormous benefits in everyday life. By far its greatest advantage is that it lets you explore the deeper levels of your inner mind and gain wisdom and real insight into life's problems and the truth about life itself.

The Spiritual Computer

Let us look at the meditative way to solve problems. There are three keywords for putting your inner mind to work:

Write — Try — Ask

Write: Write out your problem. This may sound foolish, but my experience has shown that a greater number of problems exist only because they have not been clearly defined or outlined. Once you actually write out the problem, you will find that you see it in a new light. On your paper start with the words, "Shall I do this . . . ?" Then state the problem to which you seek a solution, carefully, fully, yet concisely.

Try: Try to solve the problem yourself. On the piece of paper that states your problem, place two columns. In one column, write all the reasons for taking a particular step. In the other, list all the reasons against it.

Suppose the problem is sheer lack of money. Remember that the solution to any problem is contained within the problem itself. In other words, whatever causes the problem can cure it. The cause is always—and I stress always—within your own mind. Thoughts are powerful things, far more powerful than most people realize. What you must do, then, is to think about the problem in a particular way. Worry simply adds to the problem and shows lack of control. What is needed is control, peaceful control, as in meditation. Using the techniques already described help to bring your mind around to the problem in a positive fashion. Ask yourself: "Why am I short of money?" Your mind will then give you the obvious answers, such as loss of a job, too many debts, or not enough income. Start to look at each excuse—for that is what they are. Suppose one answer is a sheer lack of money. There simply is not enough. It does not appear to be your fault. It's just the way of things. Or is it? Go deeper and become more curious, curious to know the truth. Keep your mind on this goal—the truth. What you want is the truth about wealth. This is the solution to the problem. If you were really wealthy, there would not be any shortage of money. Ask yourself: "Why am I not wealthy?" Again the excuses will arise, but you must refuse to accept them.

You want only the truth and you know that this truth exists within your inner mind. The reason you are not wealthy is because you believe you cannot ever be wealthy. Why is it that you cannot be wealthy? Why can you never have enough? Be honest. There is no logical reason, there are only excuses. You think that wealth is for the gifted few, or that it has to be worked for. This is not true. Wealth is an attitude of mind and, as long as you listen to the excuses and believe them, you will deny yourself wealth. Of course, it is easy for me to tell you this, but it is another thing altogether to discover it for yourself as a realization. Only by doing this, by using your mind in this way, will you ever really know. Meditation affords you this chance. A calm mind in meditation will always find a solution to a problem, no matter what the problem is.

Put in enough time doing this so that you are relatively certain that you cannot solve the problem consciously. Once you are forced to reach a decision that you cannot solve the problem consciously, go to step three.

Ask: Ask your inner mind to solve the problem for you. This is the part of the procedure that many people find hard to accept. They simply cannot believe that any task of such magnitude could be carried out by simply "asking" a part of their mind to take care of it. And yet, these same people drive a car to work every morning, often becoming so involved in their own conscious thoughts that they let their inner mind do all the driving. They suddenly become aware, almost like someone awakening from sleep, that they are ready to turn off the freeway or turnpike. They are unable to recall clearly the specifics of what occurred in connection with weaving their way through traffic.

Accept it! Think of your inner mind as another person, an employee, or assistant. Just say to that force: "I want the answer to this problem by tomorrow morning." Or, if the problem is a particularly difficult one, give your mind more time. Tell it you want the answer by next Saturday, or something of the sort.

I have already spoken about the value of releasing negative thoughts in developing effective visualization. The fact of the matter is that, as soon as willpower and anxiousness are abandoned and the whole matter is allowed to turn inward and become a subjective matter, a part of the inner mind, then the process begins to work. It may continue to work, even unbeknownst to you. In other words, there must be a "releasing" of the desire and the thoughts that are formed objectively in order for the meditation to be carried out efficiently. If you try to use objective force and anxiously will the meditation to be a success, the thought itself, or the idea, is held earthbound, so to speak, in the grasp of the physical limitations of the objective aspect of the mind.

Meditation serves as an "incubation" period for problem solving and meditation. It bestows insight by letting us look at some aspect of life or some object and discover its essence. Meditation is a technique that supplies answers. It is a tool, not a mystical experience. The problem is that many practitioners simply lose themselves in masses of symbolism or seek to escape into a dream state, assuming that they have found reality. Unless the right intention is applied, however, the wrong reasons may be brought to bear, thus bringing about incorrect results. The intention governs everything, even the answers.

Much more could obviously be said about meditation, because it is a vast subject, capable of much development. I hope I have cleared away some of the misconceptions and given useful ideas to those who already practice meditation, and those who were unaware that it even existed. At the end of the meditation period, close down the cosmic sphere and return to normal.

I conclude this chapter with a practical exercise. You were introduced to the inner temple. You used colors and symbols to work with an inner temple that was "geographically" defined. In other words, you could see inside the inner temple, see the stone walls, the floor, the oak doors, and perhaps all manner of things you would find in a real physical temple. A magical inner temple is a highly individualistic affair. It is not possible for me to direct you completely. I have tried to present universal symbols, and I will try here to guide you, so you can find your own way. In other words, build your own inner temple and learn to handle that contact between yourself and your inner mind.

The validity of this structure will prove itself with regular practice. It is very important to remember that you have to work within your imagination, in an imaginary inner temple.

There are graduated exercises for coming to grips with this. The first one is very simple. Just erect the triple rings of the cosmic sphere in your imagination. The second exercise consists of entering your inner temple. One important thing that you must remember is that you must carry this new magical awareness around with you. The geographical inner temple should contain five central concepts: the four elemental gates or doors and the central pool. The idea of the pool works by becoming a valuable meditational aid. In other words, the vacuity of the pool helps you to concentrate, or rather meditate, and bring up information of a prophetic nature. If you wish to discover something, perhaps an answer to a problem, formulate this before you start your meditation ritual. When you reach the pool, "think" your question or problem into the pool. The pool can be used as a crystal ball to see into the future. It will tell you things and give you answers to questions.

The three stages of meditation are contemplation, meditation, activation. To meditate correctly, the mind must have an objective. The time during which the objective is fixed in the conscious mind is called the contemplative period, during which a link is opened to the inner mind. At this point, the inner mind takes over the search and the conscious mind is left behind until later. This is the true period of meditation, which continues until satisfaction is obtained. The truth, when found, is transferred back to the conscious mind and the final process of activation begins.

• • •

The key to the mystery of abundant living, and to life itself, is belief. As you think, so you are. Whatever you believe to be true, is true. The task is therefore to free yourself from wrong beliefs and adopt only realistic patterns of belief, thereby affecting a change in circumstances. Think poverty and you will have poverty; think wealth and it shall be yours. That is the law.

Ask yourself these three questions at the conclusion of your creative work, and during everyday life: "Am I still unconvinced that circumstances will change for the better?" If you are, they will not change. "Am I partially convinced that circumstances will get better through my efforts?" If you are, then you have set your foot upon the path of "potential" and begun to create your own reality. In due course, you will have that which you desire. "Am I totally convinced that, regardless of appearances to the contrary, I know in my heart and in my mind that circumstances will change and that I shall have whatever I desire?" If you are, you cannot fail.

Never forget that creative visualization is the art of convincing your inner mind that it must supply your designated needs, regardless of any previous beliefs or instructions it may have had to the contrary. Linked, as they are, to your conscious rational thinking mind, inner beliefs are reflected in outer habits, reactions, mannerisms, and thoughts. If you have been successful in convincing your inner mind, this will reflect itself in your everyday attitudes and thoughts. These are therefore a measure of how well the new instructions have succeeded in implanting themselves within your inner mind. Conversely, what you think and how you act is a measure of what is already within your inner mind. By looking at yourself, your thoughts, and your actions, you can therefore measure your progress.

Are you convinced?

During times of crisis, there is a disinclination to attempt creative workings of the sort given in this book. The mind is preoccupied with the possible outcome—usually in negative terms. At these times, you are faced with a choice and a supreme moment in which you can take control and learn. Any positive effort will, I assure you, have a beneficial effect, even though this may not be immediately apparent. Trials, tribulations, and even complete disasters have within them the keys to success, strange though this may seem. It is not power that causes problems. It is wrong attitudes and beliefs. When a major problem occurs, it indicates that some aspect of power is at peak flow and, because of wrong thinking, the results are obviously bad. Therefore, since thoughts dictate how energy will affect your life, it makes profound sense to take advantage of energy peaks by changing your inner thoughts at these times. Action taken while problems are most vexing is bound to be more effective than at any other time.

Here at the end of this book, you are faced with one final choice—whether to carry on as usual, hoping that fate may intervene or that lucky charms and "instant" magic books will save you from what appears to be disaster, or whether to accept the basic truths which have been presented to you. Should you decide on the latter and, more important, resolve to think about and apply these truths, you will know lasting success and realize the profound truth:

As you think—So you are

The more optimistic you are, the wider your vision and the more expansive your thoughts, the better will be the quality of your life, not only from a financial point of view, but in other areas as well. Think about your life. Think about what creative visualization can do for you and how it can improve the quality of your life in many ways. Think positively about these things and you shall have them, for that is the law. What you hold in your mind, you will have. In biblical terms, "Cast not your seed upon stony ground." Instead, plant "seed" thoughts in the fertile earth of your inner mind and the harvest of abundance will be yours.

As you sow—So shall you reap

It is my sincere desire that you will choose to walk the path of reality, wisdom, and abundance and that you will come to know the truth.

Bibliography

Bolles, Richard N. *How to Create a Picture of Your Ideal Job or Next Career*. Berkeley, CA: Ten Speed Press, 1989.

Bristol, C. *The Magic of Believing*. Englewood Cliffs, NJ: Prentice-Hall, 1957.

Cooper, Phillip. *Basic Magick: A Practical Guide*. York Beach, ME: Samuel Weiser, 1996.

———. *The Magickian: A Study in Effective Magick*. York Beach, ME: Samuel Weiser, 1993.

Faraday, Ann. *The Dream Game*. New York: Harper & Row, 1976.

Fries, Jan. *Visual Magick*. Oxford, England: Mandrake, 1992.

Gawain, Shakti. *Creative Visualization*. San Rafael, CA: New World Library, 1995.

Hill, Napoleon. *Think and Grow Rich*. Hollywood, CA: Wilshire, 1966.

Horne, Kenneth. *Somebody Said That It Couldn't Be Done*. Kings Langley, England: Paper Publications, 1995.

Laut, Phil. *Money Is My Friend*. Charlotte, NC: Vivation Publishing, 1984.

LeCron, Leslie M. *Self-Hypnosis: The Technique and Its Use in Daily Living*. New York: New American Library, 1970.

Lee, Dave. *Magical Incenses*. Sheffield, England: Revelation 23 Press, 1992.

Ophiel. *The Art and Practice of Clairvoyance*. York Beach, ME: Samuel Weiser, 1969.

———. *The Art and Practice of Contacting the Demiurge*. Oakland, CA: Peach Publications, 1978.

———. *The Art and Practice of Getting Material Things Through Creative Visualization*. York Beach, ME: Samuel Weiser, 1975. Revised edition: retitled *The Art and Practice of Creative Visualization*, 1997.

Spare, Austin O. *The Book of Pleasure: (Self Love): The Psychology of Ecstasy*. Northampton, England: Sut Anubis, 1987.

Index

Things I Need

Suggestions:	I Need:
Rent or mortgage payment	_____
New furniture	_____
Bills paid	_____
New stove	_____
Medical insurance	_____
Regular income	_____
New job	_____
New clothes	_____
Medical operation	_____
Car repair	_____
New washing machine	_____
Dental work	_____
Own apartment or house	_____
or anything necessary to	_____
satisfy your current	_____
requirements	_____

Things I Desire

Suggestions: I Desire:

New car "Mercedes"   _____

$500,000 in the bank   _____

My own business   _____

A successful marriage   _____

A world cruise   _____

A country house   _____

A luxury yacht   _____

A vacation hideaway   _____

Own property abroad   _____

To get out of debt   _____

Spend more quality time with
my family   _____

Better health   _____

_____   _____

_____   _____

Personal Qualities I Need and Desire

Suggestions: I Need and Desire:

More self-confidence   _____

To stop "putting things off"   _____

Ability to finish what I start   _____

To be in good health   _____

More original thinking-creativity   _____

To stop "wasting time"   _____

To have more courage   _____

To attract more friends   _____

To be more aggressive   _____

To have more perseverance   _____

To achieve more goals   _____

To have an excellent memory   _____

To be enthusiastic   _____

To be an excellent speaker   _____

To be the center of attention   _____

To be at ease in the company
of the opposite sex   _____

To be a leader   _____

About the Author

Phillip Cooper's creative and experimental involvement in Magick and mind power spans more than sixteen years. This includes the nature of astral projection, altered states of consciousness, and ritual sigilization. Phillip Cooper has also long been involved in Hermetic Magick in the grand tradition of the Cabala. He lives in Northampton, England, with his wife and four children. He is the author of *The Magickian: A Study in Effective Magick* (Samuel Weiser, 1993) and *Basic Magick: A Practical Guide* (Samuel Weiser, 1996).